ABU SIMBEL
A Short Guide to the Temples

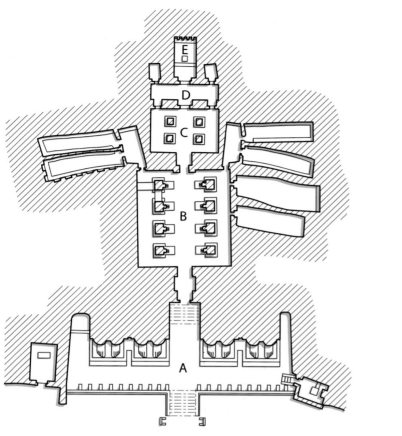

15 m

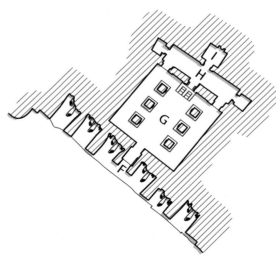

Ground plan of the two temples: (A) the Great Temple terrace
and façade; (B) the large pillared hall; (C) the small pillared hall;
(D) the vestibule; (E) the sanctuary; (F) the Small Temple façade;
(G) the pillared hall; (H) the vestibule; (I) the sanctuary.

ABU SIMBEL
A Short Guide to the Temples

Nigel Fletcher-Jones

The American University in Cairo Press
Cairo   New York

This edition first published in 2021 by
The American University in Cairo Press
113 Sharia Kasr el Aini, Cairo, Egypt
One Rockefeller Plaza, New York, NY 10020
www.aucpress.com

Copyright © 2021 by Nigel Fletcher-Jones

Extracted and condensed from *Abu Simbel and the Nubian Temples*, first published in English in 2019 by the American University in Cairo Press

Dar el Kutub No. 14480/19
ISBN 978 977 416 970 0

Dar el Kutub Cataloging-in-Publication Data

Fletcher-Jones, Nigel
      A Short Guide to Abu Simbel: English Edition/Nigel Fletcher-Jones.— Cairo: The American University in Cairo Press, 2021.
      p.   cm.
      ISBN 978 977 416 970 0
      1.   Temples—Nubia—Guidebooks
      2.   Great Temple (Abu Simbel, Egypt)—Guidebooks
      932

1 2 3 4 5   25 24 23 22 21

Designed by Sally Boylan
Printed in China

CONTENTS

Approaching Abu Simbel on Lake Nasser.

1 | UNDERSTANDING ABU SIMBEL

The rock-cut temples at Abu Simbel hold a special place in the imagination of both archaeologists and travelers.

When the discovery of the Great Temple at Abu Simbel was announced to the outside world in 1813 by the Swiss explorer Johann Ludwig Burckhardt (1784–1817), only the barest tops of the colossal statues were visible (the Small Temple had already been seen from the river by this time, and had been used for centuries by nearby villagers as an animal shelter).

Soon afterward, Giovanni Battista Belzoni (1778–1823), an Italian amateur water engineer, circus strongman, and showman-turned-explorer, acting on Burckhardt's report, cleared the way into the Great Temple (entering it on August 1, 1817) and gradually the story of Abu Simbel began to unfold.

As it was to turn out when the hieroglyphic language was deciphered a little later in the nineteenth century, what Burckhardt had found, and Belzoni had partly cleared, were temples carved on the order of one of the greatest showmen of the ancient world, Pharaoh Rameses II, who ruled approximately 1265–1200 BC.

We do not know precisely why the temples were built at Abu Simbel. No one is buried here, for example. Probably it was because the two sandstone hills were already associated with the god Horus and the goddess Hathor prior to the temples' construction, and Rameses and his senior local officials seem to have had a particular interest in temples that were excavated, or partially excavated, into riverside cliffs. This may have been linked in part to ancient Egyptian creation myths, which center around a mound or hill emerging from primeval waters.

There can be little doubt, though, that one of the purposes of the Great Temple was to intimidate the peoples nearby and those who passed along the Nile River directly in front of the temples. Vividly colored, the colossal statues of the king against the sandstone bluffs would have left quite an impression on traders heading downriver through Nubia.

The word 'Nubia' may be derived from the ancient Egyptian word *nwb*, meaning 'gold,' and Abu Simbel lies on the route along which precious African trade goods made their way to the ancient land of Egypt, whose traditional border lay at the granite shelf that impedes the Nile ('the First Cataract') at modern Aswan. There, goods would be traded on Elephantine Island (ancient Abw, part of the town known in Greek as 'Syene').

Rameses II, it appears—in this otherwise desolate place—was making a very clear statement: "You are now in Egypt and I am king and god here."

Yet there is more to Abu Simbel than that.

Together, the two temples represent one of few examples in ancient Egypt of temples constructed on the same site for both husband and wife. Rameses II had many wives and fathered perhaps 100 children in his long lifetime, yet it is not difficult to infer from the dedication of the Small Temple to his Great Wife Nefertiry (sometimes written 'Nefertari'), and from the glorious tomb that was constructed for her in the Valley of the Queens opposite ancient Thebes (Luxor), that Nefertiry was not only Great Wife but the king's favorite among many. This viewpoint is strengthened—especially given the character of Rameses II—by the appearance outside the Small Temple of colossal statues of Nefertiry that are almost the same height as those of Rameses II—though he still managed four statues, to the queen's two.

Other queens were probably represented at Abu Simbel, as were a number of royal princes and princesses, but Nefertiry held pride of place as mother of the king's firstborn son, Amenhirwenemef.

When the temples were first explored in 1817, the names and characters of the ancient Egyptian kings, gods, and goddesses were largely unknown. The earliest European visitors had read the description of Egypt by the ancient Greek historian Herodotus—who may have visited Egypt around 450 BC—and the works of other commentators from the classical Mediterranean world, so the names of major Egyptian gods such as Amun, Osiris, and Horus were at least familiar to them. Knowledge of the goddess Isis had also survived through the centuries as her cult had spread widely throughout the Greek and Roman worlds. Yet concerning many other gods and goddesses, there was only guesswork. The fearsome and ancient goddess Sekhmet, with a lion's head and a woman's body, was thought at the time by some—though not necessarily with any great conviction—to be an astrological entity combining Leo and Virgo.

While we can now identify all the gods and goddesses at Abu Simbel with confidence, we are less certain about the rituals that might have been performed there, though we can fill in many gaps from inscriptions, documents, and decoration from other temples.

Part of the reason for this inherited vagueness is that neither the Arab elite who arrived in Egypt and Nubia in AD 639–42 nor the Ottoman Turks (1517) considered ancient Egypt to be part of their cultural heritage.

Abu Simbel, from Belzoni, *Narrative of the Operations and Recent Discoveries Within the Pyramids, Temples, Tombs and Excavations in Egypt and Nubia* (London: 1820).

However, the major loss of knowledge of the pharaonic past was due to the early arrival of Christianity in Egypt—traditionally through the apostle Mark, who is said to have landed at Alexandria around AD 50. When Christianity took deep hold, there appears to have been only limited assimilation of the old religion into the new, although a few ancient traditions and festivals have survived in Egypt to the present day.

In Christian Egyptian, many temples were converted, as a whole or in part, into churches, and the images of the ancient gods and goddesses were defaced or simply covered over with plaster (which, accidentally, often preserved them for recent generations). Knowledge of the meaning of hieroglyphic inscriptions was lost, although the ancient Egyptian language itself survived in a greatly modified form in the liturgy of the Coptic Christian Church.

In ancient Nubia, the vast expanse of land that flanks the Nile from the First Cataract at Aswan 970 kilometers (600 miles) south, and within which the temples at Abu Simbel lie, the old religion survived longer than in Egypt, which became wholly Christian after the edict of the emperor Theodosius I in AD 394. The Byzantine emperor Justinian finally closed the cult at Philae, just south of Aswan, only in AD 535. Yet, ultimately, here too the old temples to the gods were either converted into churches, defaced, or simply left to the desert.

Despite this loss of a direct connection to the past, at Abu Simbel we are confident that we can correctly identify the gods associated with the temples—principally Re-Horakhty (god of the noonday sun) and Hathor (the goddess of femininity, and daughter of Re), but also King Rameses II himself, who was worshipped as a god in his own lifetime.

For at Abu Simbel Rameses II could worship himself, as he is seen doing in several places in the halls of the temples. Indeed, in the sanctuary of the Great Temple, he sits equally with Ptah (a creator god and patron god of the Egyptian capital Memphis), Amun-Re (the supreme god worshipped at Thebes), and Re-Horakhty ('Re-flying-high-within-the-horizons'), to whom the Great Temple was principally dedicated.

Famously, these four seated figures are illuminated by the sunrise twice a year on February 21/22 and October 21/22. Although much is made of this today, we simply don't know whether this was by design or just coincidence. Ancient Egyptian engineers were certainly capable of the degree of precision required to illuminate the sanctuary in this way, but there is no textual evidence to support the idea of a special meaning surrounding these dates, and the notion that there might be such a meaning only seems to have gathered ground around the time that the temples were moved to their present location in the 1960s.

Much of the decoration within the first pillared hall of the Great Temple is concerned with Rameses II's prowess in warfare. He can be seen in various poses vanquishing his enemies. On the left-hand walls, 'Libyans'—from the northwest boundary of the ancient Egyptian state—are defeated alongside Syrians and Hittites, a people from Anatolia (now central Turkey), both northeast of Egypt. The all-powerful king also subjugates Nubians from the southern border. These are familiar decorations in the temples built by Rameses II (and his predecessors and successors), as is some part of the narrative of the battle of Qadesh (Kadesh), that occupies the whole right-hand wall of the first pillared hall in the Great Temple in almost comic-strip fashion.

The battle of Qadesh was clearly a never-surpassed moment in Rameses II's life. Following in the footsteps of his father Sethy I (reigned about 1276–1265 BC),

The sun illuminating the large pillared hall, Great Temple.

he tried to secure this strategic city in Syria against the forces of the Hittite empire, which had spread out from their Anatolian homelands to threaten Egyptian interests in the region. The story of the battle, told in detail from the Egyptian perspective in multiple locations across Egypt, is riveting, and naturally focuses on the role of the pharaoh. That the battle was at best a draw, and that Qadesh remained in Hittite hands afterward, does not enter into the Egyptian narrative. The emphasis is always on what appears to have been the genuine personal bravery of the Egyptian king in preventing a rout and achieving a glorious 'victory.'

In both temples, any warlike emphasis is left behind in the outer hall. This is consistent with the general pattern of ancient Egyptian temples, that—from the outside to the inside—represent the transition from chaos to order, from light to darkness, and from the human plane to the divine.

In the second pillared hall of the Great Temple, and beyond toward the sanctuary—areas that would have normally been inaccessible to all but the professional priests and their attendants who performed rituals before the gods in the king's stead— the central theme is that of the closeness of the king to the gods and goddesses who were ever-present in Egyptian life, and the king's ability to appease and communicate with them, sometimes as their equal, and sometimes as less than that.

In the vestibule of each temple, three times a day—in the morning, at midday, and in the evening— offerings of food and drink would be presented to the principal gods of the temple by the senior or high priest, junior priests, and attendants.

At the same time, the high priest would break the seals on the doors to the sanctuary and enter, probably alone, to ritually attend the gods, who were thought to reside in some manner, and perhaps only at this time, in the painted statues carved from the bare rock of the hills. The rituals would have at least included prayers and the extensive use of incense.

When the rituals were complete, all trace of the sanctuary having been entered would have been removed, and the doors resealed.

Peace would return to the temples.

About This Book

This brief book is intended to serve as a guide, so the visitor can find out more about what is important about the temples before they enter, or while they are there.

In explaining what is important about the temples, I have kept the archaeological and Egyptological jargon to a minimum, but where it cannot be entirely avoided, I have tried to explain terms immediately.

A Note Concerning Dates

Prior to about 690 BC, there are no exact dates of events in ancient Egyptian history.

In their writings, the ancient Egyptians measured the annual passing of time by 'regnal years'—the number of years the current king had sat on the throne. Thus, throughout this book, an event in the life of Rameses II will be no more precisely dated than 'in the xx year of his reign' or 'in Year xx.'

Around the year 300 BC, Manetho, an Egyptian priest, writing in Greek, attempted to bring order to the long royal history of ancient Egypt by grouping kings into 30 dynasties based on the familial or political ties of pharaohs. Perhaps needless to say, there have been arguments about this list ever since: another dynasty has been tacked on to the end; we believe some listed kings probably did not exist; and some, who we know from the archaeological record did exist, aren't present in the list. This does not provide a very firm basis for establishing the reigns of pharaohs with any degree of precision.

So, while the dates of the reign of Rameses II are described here as 1265–1200 BC, the reader may also see the spans 1290–1223 (for example) and 1279–1212 BC stated in other books with equal conviction. In the great timespan of the Egyptian state, such a tiny discrepancy must surely be forgivable.

For the record, Rameses II was a member of the Nineteenth Dynasty, which began when his grandfather Rameses I, a former general, became king around 1278 BC and lasted until the end of the reign of the female king Tawosret around 1176 BC.

Unsurprisingly, the Nineteenth Dynasty followed the Eighteenth Dynasty (around 1540–1278 BC), which was one of the most successful, and then one of the most turbulent, periods of ancient Egyptian history. Some of the most familiar pharaohs belonged to this dynasty, including (the female king) Hatshepsut, Akhenaten, and Tutankhamun.

Egyptologists include both of these dynasties in a broader convenient subdivision of Egypt's long history, the New Kingdom, which lasted from about 1540 BC to around 1078 BC.

These broader divisions start with the formation of the Egyptian state in the *Early Dynastic Period* (approximately 2900–2580 BC), followed by the *Old Kingdom* (2580–2120 BC); an unsettled period known as the *First Intermediate Period* (2120–2010 BC); the *Middle Kingdom* (2010–1660 BC); another unsettled period known as the *Second Intermediate Period* (1660–1540 BC); the *New Kingdom* (1540–1078 BC); the *Third Intermediate Period* (1078–664 BC); the *Saite Period* (664–525 BC, named after the city of Sais in the western Delta where pharaohs made their capital); and the *Late Period* (525–332 BC), which saw the increasing involvement of the Persians until they took control of Egypt directly in 342 BC. The Persians were defeated in 332 BC by Alexander the Great, who inaugurated the *Hellenistic Period* (332–30 BC, including the rule of the Greek Ptolemies), which lasted until the *Roman Period* of 30 BC to AD 395.

These divisions are useful while looking at the grand scale of ancient Egyptian history, but as no self-respecting ancient Egyptian woke up during the reign of Rameses II thinking of himself as living in the Nineteenth Dynasty within the New Kingdom, I have used the more familiar BC and AD framework (sometimes written elsewhere as BCE and CE) and year of the king's reign throughout this book.

2 | THE GREAT AND SMALL TEMPLES

Rameses II was both a prolific builder of new temples and a modifier of those built by his predecessors. His name, in the form of a cartouche (a royal name in hieroglyphs inside an oval shape with a line at one end), appears all over Egypt, often carved so deeply that it would be very difficult for any kingly successor to remove it, though in the centuries to come, some managed the task.

A number of temples were built, completed, or modified in Lower Nubia (the northern part of Nubia—immediately south of Aswan) during his reign, including Beit al-Wali, Gerf Hussein, Wadi al-Sebua, Derr, and Abu Simbel—of which the most justly celebrated, and the ones in which he was most heavily involved in the planning and execution, are the Great and Small Temples at Abu Simbel.

The purpose of the Nubian temples was mixed. They must have served as propaganda—intimidating the Nubian population and passing traders by proclaiming Egyptian superiority—but they also appear to have shown, through their depiction of local forms of gods and goddesses, a willingness by the Egyptian state to adapt to local conditions and beliefs in order to 'assimilate' its southern neighbor. We can, perhaps, see this in the ubiquitous presence of Amun in the temples—especially in the Great Temple—directly associated with the Nubian temple to Amun at Gebel Barkal far to the south (in modern Sudan), and in the consistent presence of the divine trio, the god Khnum and the goddesses Anukis and Satis, whose cult center was on Elephantine Island in Aswan (see chapter three for brief descriptions of the main gods and goddesses associated with the Abu Simbel temples).

By this period, Egyptian temples followed a more or less standardized plan and were either fully or partially cut into rock faces, or freestanding. Rameses II seems to have had a preference for the fully or partially rock-cut temple in Nubia—the gods in the sanctuary, at the furthest point from the door, being

The exterior of the Great Temple.

carved from the rock, then plastered and painted. This aspect of temple architecture may be related to an Egyptian creation myth in which the gods lived and came into the world from a primeval mound. In the same way, in the case of partially rock-cut temples, the outer part may have been deliberately intended to symbolize the human world and the excavated interior the divine.

The location of Rameses II's rock-cut Nubian temples may also have been determined by a symbolic southward journey of the pharaoh while worshipping the sun god, Re, the primary god of both Egypt and Nubia.

The extent to which this possible pattern was part of a 'master plan' is unknown, particularly as some of the temples were built by the king and others in his honor by his viceroys (governors) in Nubia.

All the rock-cut temples broadly share the same architectural features: a 'pylon' (the monumental entrance traditionally consisting of two towers with backward-sloping fronts, and a door in the middle) or gate, with colossal statues of the king on either side; a first hall containing pillars or an open court that often led into a second hall containing pillars; then, usually, a vestibule (a room where rituals took place and offerings were made before reaching the sanctuary); and, at the rear of the temple, three rooms—the central one being the sanctuary of the god or gods to whom the temple was dedicated. Most temples, as at Abu Simbel, had additional storerooms for offerings, or possibly tribute to the king from the Nubian population.

To enhance the focus on the sanctuary, temple rooms tended to become smaller as it was approached, and the floor was made to slope upward and the ceiling downward slightly. The temples were also designed so that while full sunlight might cover the entrance, only a minimum of light could enter the sanctuary.

The reliefs associated with Lower Nubian temples are essentially of two types: military scenes of the king smiting Egypt's enemies (thus maintaining the security of the state and keeping the forces of chaos at bay), which are usually found on the outside walls and in the first hall; and scenes in which the king interacts with the gods (thus maintaining order and security for the people), which are usually found in the inner rooms toward the sanctuary. All the scenes and statues would have been plastered and brightly colored—principally in Rameses II's favorite bold palette of black, red, and yellow.

Military scenes on the north wall tend to depict battles in the north, and scenes on the south wall tend to depict battles in the south. These scenes were not intended necessarily to convey historical events, with the notable exception of the often-repeated representation in the temples built by Rameses II of the battle of Qadesh, which occurred early in Rameses's reign.

In all the Nubian temples, Rameses II can be found worshipping himself in the fully developed form of a god (his 'deified' self). He may, in part, have copied this aspect of self-worship from the

Nubian temples of Amenhotep III (also known by the Greek name Amenophis III, who reigned around 1377–1337 BC) to the south at Soleb—though this concept had emerged earlier in ancient Egyptian history in the reign of the female king Hatshepsut. Interestingly, Amenhotep III had also built a temple to his principal wife, Tiye, at Sedeinga, where she took the form of the goddesses Hathor and Tefnut. For many reasons, it seems reasonable to suggest, in any case, that Rameses II thought of Amenhotep III as something of a kingly role model.

The Great Temple

The Great Temple at Abu Simbel was carved 60 meters (200 feet) into a hill that was already sacred to Horus of Maha (a localized form of the god Horus).

The temple was dedicated principally to the god Re-Horakhty (whose worship was centered at Heliopolis, near the modern Cairo suburb), with Amun-Re (whose main center of worship was at Thebes, modern Luxor), Rameses II in the form of a god, and the god Ptah (whose cult center was at Memphis, southeast of modern Cairo, near the pyramids at Saqqara) in supporting roles.

At a place judged appropriate by the architects and priests, the rock face was cut back to resemble the pylon (backward-sloping gate with two towers and a central gate) of a freestanding temple. The entrance to Luxor temple—also surrounded by colossal statues of Rameses II—gives a good idea of what was intended in imitation.

The two towers of a pylon may have represented watchtowers keeping intruders and the chaotic everyday world at bay, and pylons also appear to mimic the shape of the *akhet* or horizon hieroglyph ⌂ signifying the importance of sunlight in the design of the temple. For while sunlight might bathe the pylon, the hidden elements of the inner temple were protected from the sun's rays.

This role of sunlight can be seen best at dawn at Abu Simbel as the line of light starts down the face of the temple.

First, the line of baboons—traditional greeters of the rising sun—are illuminated.

Then two lines of hieroglyphs are lit. The top line consists of the cartouches of the king with a cobra on either side. The second line consists of the titles of the king running away from the center. Here Rameses is identified with the god Horus, and as the Strong Bull of Egypt: "Live Horus," the inscription says. "The Strong Bull Beloved of Truth. King of Upper and Lower Egypt. Powerful in Justice is Re. Chosen of Re. Son of Re. Rameses, Beloved of Amun." The inscription continues on the south (left) side: "Beloved of Amun-Re, King of the Gods," and on the north (right) side: "Beloved of Re-Horakhty, the Great God."

Next, the heads of the 21-meter (69-foot) colossal statues of Rameses are lit, showing the double crown of Upper and Lower Egypt and the sacred rearing cobra (uraeus ♆) in front of the striped *nemes* head cloth. Between the two sets of royal heads stands a statue of Re-Horakhty ('Re-flying-high-within-the-horizons') surmounted by a solar disk.

In his right hand, Re-Horakhty holds the jackal-headed sign for power *(user)* and, in his left, the figure of the goddess of truth and justice, Maat. Together, this spells out part of the throne name taken by Rameses II on his accession: 'User-maat-Re' ('the justice of Re is powerful,' in full 'Usermaatre-Setpenre'—adding 'Chosen of Re'). On either side, Rameses II can be seen offering a figure of Maat (𓁏) to Re-Horakhty and to his own name.

Each of the colossal statues has a name inscribed on the king's shoulder proclaiming different aspects of Rameses II. From left to right they are 'The Sun of the Rulers,' 'The Ruler of the Two Lands,' 'The Beloved of Amun,' and 'The Beloved of Atum.'

On either side, at just below knee height on the colossi, the sun shines on new statues. These are members of the king's family, including his oldest children—which leads us to believe that the

Above the doorway, Re-Horakhty holds the *user* symbol in his right hand, and the *maat* symbol of truth and justice in his left hand, spelling out the throne name of Rameses II, User-maat-Re ('the justice of Re is powerful').

Queen Nefertiry stands beside the first northern colossal statue of Rameses II.

construction of the temple began around the fifth year of Rameses' reign.

The southernmost colossus has statues of Rameses II's daughters: Nebettawy, an unnamed daughter, and Bintanat. To the right, the second colossus has statues of Rameses' mother Tuy, his first-born son Amenhirwenemef, and the latter's mother, Rameses II's first (co-)Great Wife, Nefertiry.

Across the main entrance, Nefertiry appears again, with Prince Rameses and another daughter, Bakmut. Lastly, by the most northerly statue, the Queen Mother Tuy appears for the second time, with Princess Meryetamun, and her mother, Nefertiry. The whole façade was thus a monument to the entire royal family, a concept seemingly introduced for the first time in the Nineteenth Dynasty.

At about this stage of the sunrise, sunlight would enter the temple through the doorway, but for most of the year, it would not penetrate very far. However, twice each year the sunlight would penetrate the whole of the temple and illuminate the sanctuary.

Finally, in front of the colossi lies a terrace, with a line of alternating statues of Rameses II and falcons representing Re-Horakhty. These are the last to be lit by the rising sun.

During Rameses II's reign, the Great Temple could probably only be approached from the river. Continuous mud-brick walls—partially reconstructed on the north side today—blocked the way, apart from the stone gate that led to the Small Temple.

It is possible that even the lowliest traveler or villager might have been able to offer prayers or ask for the intercession of the gods within this outer area, or perhaps they might have been permitted to do so

The terrace of the Great Temple with alternating statues of Rameses II and falcons representing Re-Horakhty.

only at certain times of the year. Those prayers might have been focused on the colossal statues of Rameses II, as appears to have happened in Thebes (Luxor), where the colossal statues of the king had their own assigned priests.

Whoever they might be, visitors to the temple could cross the forecourt toward the terrace, though there was also a small temple to the left of the Great Temple, which contains reliefs of Thoth and Re-Horakhty and may have been a way station for the sacred small boats (barques or barks) associated with worship in the temple. To the right of the Great Temple, there is another small open court temple associated with the sun god.

As they approached the terrace steps, they would pass two freestanding inscription stones (stelae) and two basins set aside for ritual washing by the temple priests. The inscription stone (stela) on the left showed the king offering incense to the gods Amun-Re, Ptah, and Isis; the one on the right showed the king offering flowers to Amun-Re, Re-Horakhty, and Thoth.

There are a number of other stelae that might interest our visitors on the terrace in passing, but the one that would catch most of their attention is an inscription in the southernmost corner at the front of the terrace. It records the arrangements, in Year 34 of Rameses II's reign, for the marriage of a Hittite princess to Rameses, who can just be seen at the top receiving the princess (in Egyptian dress) and her father King Hattusilis III. Paraphrased freely, the inscription says:

Then the chief of the land of Kheta [the Egyptian name for Hatti, the land of the Hittites] spoke to his army and his nobles saying: "Our land is devastated. . . . We have been taken captive with all our possessions; my eldest daughter being the first among them. . . ."

Then they came with their possessions, their splendid gifts of silver and gold, and many great marvels. . . .

[Messengers came] to the delight of his majesty, saying: "Behold, the great chief of Kheta is coming, bringing his eldest daughter, bearing much tribute. Everything! They have crossed many mountains and difficult roads, so they might reach the boundaries of his majesty's country."

His majesty received the news [of their coming] in the palace with joy in his heart. When he heard of such strange and unexpected events, he commanded [a guard of honor] and his sons to go quickly and receive [the Hittite king].

His army came back [quickly], their legs being strong, and their stride long, and the daughter of the great chief of Kheta marched in front of the army.

The great chiefs of every other country came too; they were all intimidated, turning away in fright, when they saw his majesty, the king of Kheta, come with them to seek the favor of King Rameses.

The large pillared hall of the Great Temple.

As we shall see later, the apparent surprise of Rameses II at the marriage party's arrival within the Egyptian borders would probably only have been surpassed by Hattusilis III's surprise to find that his land was described as devastated and that he was bringing tribute to the pharaoh as his conqueror.

Returning to the entrance to the temple, the most important of our visitors might begin, perhaps, to make the transition from the outside world of sunlight to a darker world inside.

There were reminders in the entrance passageway of the king's power to vanquish the traditional enemies of Egypt: bound captive Nubians on the left wall; 'Libyan' captives and prisoners from among the peoples (referred to as 'Asiatics') to the northeast of Egypt on the right wall. Here too were reminders of the unity of the country as represented by the king: Nile gods tie the lotus and the papyrus—representing Upper and Lower Egypt—together around the hieroglyph meaning 'unite.'

Finally crossing the threshold, our most privileged ancient Egyptian visitors would leave the outside world behind.

The first pillared hall contains eight statues of Rameses II in the form of the god of the underworld, Osiris. His arms are crossed on his chest and he holds the crook and flail, symbols of power. The statues on the left wear the Upper Egyptian crown ( ), and those on the right wear the double crown of Upper and Lower Egypt ( ). To the rear and sides of each statue are images of Rameses II, Nefertiry, and Princess Bintanat making offerings to the gods.

Between the last two statues on the left side (looking toward the sanctuary) stands a stela recording the gifts and buildings dedicated by Rameses to the great temple of Ptah at Memphis (the ancient capital of Egypt, 20 kilometers [12 miles] south of Giza).

It is a particularly lengthy and flowery inscription, but it gives some idea of the great building work done by Rameses II in the ancient capital. Paraphrased again, it says in part:

I have enlarged your house in Memphis, protecting it with everlasting works. With great labor—using building blocks, gold, and expensive stones—I have constructed your forecourt to the north of the temple with a magnificent double façade. The doors are like the horizon of heaven, causing even strangers to praise you. I made for you a magnificent temple in the middle of the enclosure. [The divine image of you,] god, which I have fashioned, is in its secret chapel, resting upon its great throne.

Even in the low level of light, the colors in this hall would have stood out. The palette was dominated by red, yellow, and black—the first two made from local ochre deposits and the last from soot and charcoal.

Above, vultures fly across the ceiling of the center aisle, separated by the cartouche of the king (now faded); the ceilings of the side aisles are painted with stars.

The walls of the first pillared hall are dominated by images of Rameses II as the military protector of the Egyptian state.

Traditional scenes of the king smiting enemies before Amun-Re (south side) and Re-Horakhty (north side) appear on either side of the door on the inside of the temple, while a line of royal children appears underneath—royal princes on the right when facing the entrance (south), royal princesses on the left (north). Under the princesses, there is a rare signature of one of the original sculptors of the temple, named Piay, in four columns of hieroglyphs.

Although the long reign of Rameses II seems to have been relatively peaceful after the first few years, the left (south) wall of the first pillared hall is dominated by unnamed campaigns against Syrians, Libyans, and Nubians. Some of these campaigns

Vultures representing the protective goddess Nekhbet fly across the ceiling of the first pillared hall, separated by the faded cartouche of Rameses II.

Rameses II attacks an unnamed Syrian fortress together with three sons (to the right of this scene). The king's extra arms and bows are the result of artist's corrections which would have been plastered over: east end of the south wall, large pillared hall.

were almost certainly imaginary—the overarching theme here was simply the projection of the military prowess of the king in keeping the enemies of the state at bay.

Images of the pharaoh ritually destroying the enemies of the state stretch back to Egypt's earliest times (for example, on the Narmer palette, dated to around 3000 BC) and also form part of the consistent plan of Egyptian temples from the entrance to the sanctuary: from light to darkness; from the human world to the divine; and from chaos to order under the king, through his military prowess and through his intimate relationship with the gods. Descent back into the chaos from which the primitive world had emerged was regarded as inevitable by the ancient Egyptians, and it could only be held at bay through the mediation

The king spears a Libyan chieftain while treading on a
fallen warrior: middle of the south wall, large pillared hall.

The Great Temple   21

of the king and—on his behalf—the priesthood within
the temples. Chaos and order, naturally, were always
bound to be a preoccupation in a land where the
desert (representing chaos) continually pressed against
the thin strip of agricultural land at the edges of the
Nile (representing order and stability).

At the east (left) end of the south wall, Rameses,
in all his glory, is seen in a chariot attacking a Syrian
fortress, accompanied by three of his sons. On close
inspection, the king appears today to have two bows
and extra arms—the effect of an alteration made in
the original carving that would have been invisible
when originally plastered over and painted.

Halfway along the same wall is a dramatic image
of the king spearing a Libyan chieftain—a copy of
a relief created for Rameses' father Sethy I (reigned
1276–1265 BC) on the outer wall of the Great
Hypostyle Hall at Karnak temple. To the right again,
Rameses appears in his chariot—accompanied by his
pet lion—driving Nubians before him toward the
gods on the next wall on the right.

Above these warlike scenes, the king can be seen
making offerings to several gods—on the left, incense
to Merymutef and the lion-headed goddess Ipt, and
cloth to Amun-Re. In the middle, Thoth and Seshat
write while, next to this, the king kneels under a
sacred tree in front of Re-Horakhty as Thoth appears
again writing upon its leaves.

At the furthest right, the king appears before
the god Amun, who is emerging from the sacred
mountain at Gebel Barkal, 420 kilometers (260
miles) to the south of Abu Simbel—a nod, perhaps,

by the builders to local Nubian religious beliefs and
sensibilities. Gebel Barkal is an isolated sandstone
mountain, reminiscent of the primeval mound—the
first land that emerged at the beginning of creation—
with a separate pinnacle that resembles a rearing
cobra wearing a sun disc or white crown, depending
on the angle of view. A complex group of temples
sacred to Amun developed there from at least the
time of Thutmose III (reigned 1468–1415 BC) and
served as the place of worship of the southern form
of the god Amun of Karnak.

In the scenes on either side of the doorway,
Rameses is presenting prisoners to the gods: Nubian
captives to Amun-Re, the deified Rameses II (that is,
himself as a god), and the goddess Mut to the left (or
south side); and Hittite captives to Re-Horakhty, the
deified Rameses, and the goddess Iusaas to the right
(or north side).

The figure of the deified Rameses has clearly been
inserted at a later time among the figures to the left of
the door (and elsewhere in the temple). The goddess
Mut had originally been seated behind Amun-Re, and
the insertion of Rameses II caused the goddess to be
re-carved standing.

The deified Rameses in the inserted carving is
represented with the ram's horns of the god Amun.
This may reflect native Nubian belief involving a
ram-headed god associated with fertility and water,
later adopted in Nubia as a characteristic of the local
version of Amun, as seen extensively at the ancient
town of Kerma, 355 kilometers (220 miles) to the
south of Abu Simbel.

The god Amun emerges from the sacred Nubian mountain at Gebel Barkal: west side of the south wall, large pillared hall.

High above the door is a double scene of the king before a sphinx. On the lintel are scenes of Rameses running toward Amun-Re and Mut and, to the right, toward Re-Horakhty. On the doorjambs, he is making offerings to the gods Min, Atum, Ptah, and Montu.

The entire north wall of the great hall is taken up with a representation of the battle of Qadesh (a town on the Orontes River south of Lake Homs in Syria) against the Hittite empire, which was a defining event in the life of Rameses II and is widely represented in the temples that the pharaoh modified or had built—including at Abydos, Luxor, and his memorial temple on the west bank at Thebes, the Ramesseum.

Qadesh is the first battle in antiquity that we can reconstruct from the written record. However, such reconstruction has to be made with care, as the record is inevitably biased, and was not intended to serve as 'history' in the modern sense, but as propaganda for the king. The extent of the self-declared Egyptian victory at Qadesh is certainly open to question.

Elsewhere in Egypt, the record of the battle is composed of three parts: reliefs, a formal account (known as the Official Report), and a more flowery account (known as the Literary Record). At Abu Simbel, the Literary Record is absent and the Official Report curtailed, either due to lack of space or because it was assumed that very few people nearby would be able to read the text.

As a result, the course of the battle is illustrated here with a high degree of visual detail.

The battle itself, which occurred only a few years after Rameses II became king, was principally a clash of chariot forces supported, when possible, by infantry. The Egyptian chariotry and infantry can be seen on the move to the left of the storeroom door furthest from the entrance. Starting between the storeroom doors, the Egyptian camp near Qadesh, surrounded by shields, has been set up around the tent of the pharaoh.

Higher up, and above a frieze of the two chariot forces fighting, which stretches across the whole wall, the city of Qadesh can be seen—surrounded by the Orontes River and a canal—alongside other images of the fighting.

Much of the scene to the right of the second storeroom door (closest to the entrance) is devoted to the beginning and end of the battle. Here the young king is seen on his campstool wearing the blue war crown (*khepresh*) and discussing tactics with his officers.

Below this scene, captured Hittite spies are being interrogated, and above this scene, at the end of the battle—which continues to be waged in the margins of the wall—Hittite prisoners are rounded up as scribes count the severed hands of the enemy dead, in order to tally the slaughter and the magnitude of the Egyptian victory.

The 'defeated' Hittite king appears to the right of the city of Qadesh looking back at the city as his charioteer helps him make his escape.

In reality, the battle of Qadesh was at best a draw. Rameses II was forced to withdraw from the walls of the city and return to Egypt, while the Hittite empire remained in possession of Qadesh. It was never again to be part of the Egyptian empire.

The storerooms that cut into the Qadesh scene contain a variety of scenes of the king making offerings to gods and goddesses, as well as rock-cut shelves. These rooms—together with those entered to the left and right of the wall dividing the first and second halls—would have been used to store temple goods and, possibly, tribute from the Nubian population.

On the left, at the end of the first storeroom from the entrance on the north wall, is an unfinished image that illustrates how all the reliefs in the temple were created: the artist has marked out the outline in black ink, and the sculptor has started to chip out the rough relief, which would have been smoothly plastered and painted.

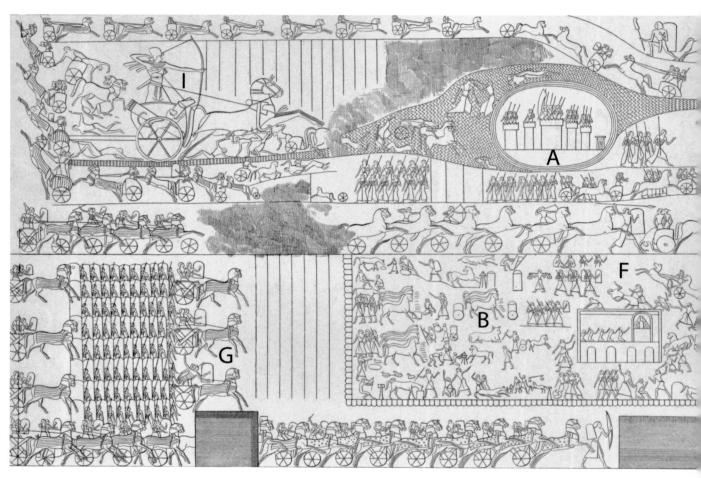

The Qadesh wall as recorded by Champollion in 1828–29. (A) the city of Qadesh surrounded by the Orontes River and canals; (B) the Egyptian camp and the royal tent set up close to Qadesh; (C) Hittite spies are beaten into revealing the close proximity of Hittite forces; (D) Rameses, wearing the blue war crown, in council with his officers and officials; (E) a messenger rides south to bring up the rest of the Egyptian army; (F) the camp is attacked; (G) a fresh division of Egyptian infantry and chariotry arrives from the west; (H) the Hittite chariot forces are repulsed; (I) the Egyptian army, led by Rameses, forces the Hittites back to the river; (J) the Hittite king leaves the battle; (K) Rameses appears in triumph as the hands of the Hittite dead are counted and prisoners are presented.

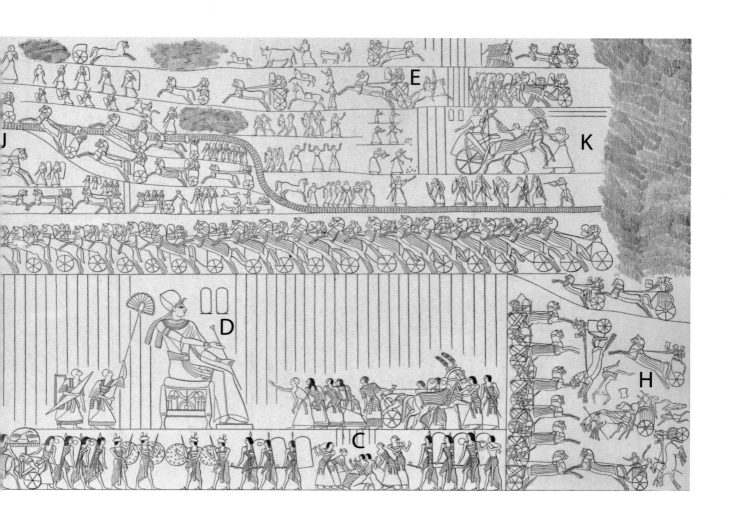

Opposite: Both the Hittite charioteers and their horses are targets for the Egyptian bowmen: lower right of the north wall.

The city of Qadesh surrounded by the Orontes River and canals: high middle of the north wall, first pillared hall.

Returning to the entrance and looking toward the sanctuary, the inevitable foreshortening involved in a rock-cut temple makes the rise in the floor toward the interior more noticeable than it would be in a similar freestanding temple. The ceiling also becomes lower, and the distance between the walls narrows, so that the eye is increasingly focused on the sanctuary.

The doors to the second pillared hall and beyond would, most probably and most of the time, remain closed to all but the priests. To make this point clearly, a sandstone falcon-headed sphinx on either side protected this doorway. These were removed by Belzoni in 1817 and are now in the British Museum.

We do not know how many priests and attendants would have been associated with the temples at Abu Simbel, but even here in the provinces, the total number of people involved in the running of the temples would have been considerable.

Any trace of their mud-brick homes had long since disappeared by the time professional archaeologists became interested in the site. The only known traces of the priestly community were rock-cut tombs discovered in the 1930s about 2 kilometers (just over a mile) to the south of the Great Temple. In addition to the priests, there would have been workmen of all

The small pillared hall of the Great Temple, where the king is greeted by and interacts with gods and goddesses.

kinds nearby to maintain the temples, and farmers to supply food for offerings to the gods and to sustain the community. Part of the endowment of the temples would certainly have included agricultural land and other valuable resources, not necessarily particularly close to the temples.

Except for very important occasional visitors, only priests and senior attendants would have crossed the threshold into the second pillared hall. This is considerably smaller than the first pillared hall and is divided into only three parts by four square pillars. The warlike imagery is not present here, as we have truly entered the ritual space of the temple.

These pillars are surrounded on all sides by images of the king being greeted by the gods—including, on the south side of the first pillar on the right, himself.

To either side of the door, the king offers flowers (symbols of life and regeneration) or lettuces (regarded in ancient Egypt as an aphrodisiac, and a phallic symbol of the fertility god Min) to the gods (Amun-Re, Mut, and himself, inserted later) to the left as the hall is entered, and to Min-Amun, Isis, and himself to the right.

On the left (south) wall, Rameses and Nefertiry make offerings in front of the sacred barque of Amun-Re; on the north wall, the king and queen do the same in front of the barque of the deified Rameses II.

These model boats—containing a statue of a god and carried by priests—were real objects. For just as the sun god Re was known to travel across the celestial sea each day by boat, so the boat was assumed to be the natural means of transportation for all gods.

The sacred barque would be carried in procession by priests particularly during festivals, sometimes being transported further on full-sized sacred boats if it was necessary for the god to be transported along

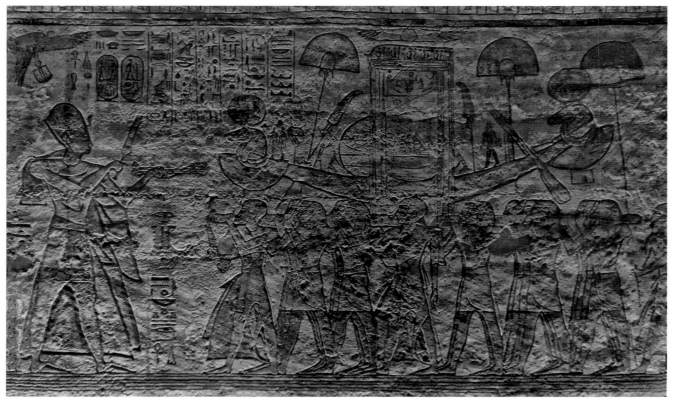

The king makes an offering of incense before the sacred barque of Amun-Re: south wall, second pillared hall.

the river. The barque of Amun at Karnak, for example, was transported in this manner to the temples along the west bank in two great processional routes—the Opet festival (along the east bank of the Nile) and the Beautiful Feast of the Valley (over on the west bank).

At the rear of the small pillared hall, three doors open to the vestibule—the central door being in line with the sanctuary (on the pillar to the left of the central door the king appears before Amun-Re; on the pillar to the right, the king appears before Re-Horakhty). These doors lead to the most sacred area of the temple, entered only by the highest ranks of the attendant priesthood, by the king, or possibly by his highest local representative.

The vestibule of the Great Temple.

The function of the vestibule is evident from the images on the wall. Here the king offers wine, incense, bread, *maat* (a small figure of the goddess representing truth, order, harmony, morality, and justice and embodying the responsibilities of the king), and flowers to the gods.

Immediately after passing through the door, and looking back toward the entrance, the king offers bread to Atum on the left partition wall, and wine to Min-Amun-Kamutef on the right. On the wall to the left of the entrance door to the sanctuary, the king offers incense to the ram-headed Amun-Re and offers flowers to Ptah to the right of the door. On the north (right-hand) wall the king offers *maat* to Thoth, and, on the south wall, wine to Horus-Ha.

Yet to fully understand the function of the vestibule, we must delve further into the ritual function of the temple, and particularly its priesthood.

Perhaps at no time in history have the concepts of religion and kingship been so deeply intertwined as they were in ancient Egypt. The king was positioned between the gods and the Egyptian people and acted on behalf of the people in relation to the gods and on behalf of the gods in relation to the people. This relationship permeated all strata of society from the very highest to the very lowest. As the Greek historian Herodotus famously remarked about the Egyptians, "They are religious excessively beyond all other men."

Although the life of the king was very deeply embedded in the most important festivals at the most important cult centers, in theory every ritual conducted in any temple in Egypt was done in the king's name and on his behalf. The king's personal and intimate role in the rituals was most often depicted on the walls—as here in the vestibule and sanctuary of the Great Temple—while the physical rituals were conducted by priests and attendants acting for him.

Although in previous centuries the priesthood was often a part-time occupation—members of the state administration serving as priests only for a few months of the year—by the time the temples at Abu Simbel were created the priesthood had become mostly professional, and often hereditary.

Strict standards of purity and cleanliness were required of priests. They were circumcised and usually required to shave their heads and keep their bodies hairless, cut their nails frequently, wash many times a day, and perform other ritual purifications, including chewing natron salt for inner cleanliness. They could not wear leather or wool but only pure linen, and, while ancient Egyptian priests were not celibate, sex rendered them unclean until purified, as did eating certain proscribed foods.

It was such priests, and their attendants, who would enter the vestibule at Abu Simbel three times a day to make offerings to the gods within the sanctuary. Here an elaborate meal would be laid out, probably on an altar or on several altars. This meal—the components of which were possibly stored in the two plain storerooms to the left and right of the sanctuary—might consist of ox, goat, or cow meat, bread, vegetables (such as onions and leeks), fruit (dates, figs, and pomegranates), and drinks including water, milk, wine, and—that great Egyptian staple—beer (often served in matching jars

The sanctuary of the Great Temple.

representing Upper and Lower Egypt). This meal was placed outside the sanctuary in its natural state, not as a burnt offering.

After the gods had enjoyed the opportunity to take such divine nourishment as they needed, the food offerings would be regarded as having returned to their natural state and were taken away to be distributed to the priests and attendants of the temple. This ritual would be repeated in the morning, at midday, and in the evening of each day (the last two 'meals' probably being reduced forms of the first).

The ultimate focus of all activity in the temple was the sanctuary. Only the high priest or the ritually purified king could enter here. When the offering meals were prepared, the high priest—perhaps with

The rock-cut images of the sanctuary. Left to right: Ptah, Amun-Re, Rameses II, and Re-Horakhty.

an attendant or two—would break the seal on the doors, and prostrate himself before the gods.

Singing hymns of adoration, he would circle the shrine or sacred boat with incense, wash and anoint the statues, and make a direct presentation of Maat in statue form. This presentation symbolically represented the king's responsibility to maintain order but also emphasized—since both the goddess Maat and the king were regarded as children of Re— his ability to do so through his special relationship with the gods.

This was the supreme offering that was seen as incorporating all other offerings. As one version of the daily ritual put it, "Maat is present in all your dwellings so that you are furnished with Maat. The robe for your limbs is Maat. Maat is breath from your nose." By presenting Maat, the priests, on behalf of the king, supplied the needs of the gods but also assisted the king in renewing and strengthening the whole fabric of the universe.

The statues in the sanctuary may have been washed and anointed with oils. Incense (known as 'the smell of the gods') would have been burned liberally. Finally, the footprints or any other mark of the presence of the high priest would be swept away and the doors of the sanctuary resealed.

Unsurprisingly, the reliefs on the sanctuary walls feature the king. On the south wall, he is again seen before the barque of Amun-Re and, on the north wall, before the barque of himself as a god.

However, the main features of the sanctuary are the altar upon which the sacred barque or shrine rested and the four life-sized statues against the west wall: from left to right, Ptah, Amun-Re, the deified Rameses II, and Re-Horakhty. These cult images, though cut from the rock, were regarded as living beings—the gods were present in them during the rituals and could be addressed by mortals. Twice a year—on February 21/22 and October 21/22—these statues are illuminated by the rising sun with the exception of Ptah, the ancient self-created god, lord of Memphis, the patron of craftsmen, and the lord of truth.

Although Ptah, when not combined with another god (such as Osiris), was not often associated with the afterlife, it may be that this lack of illumination was an intentional reminder of this association with the underworld. In any case, the dimly lit appearance of the god may have been a sufficient connection to the funerary and afterlife characteristics of the god to be understood.

Although the architects of the period were capable of producing this spectacle, there is nothing in the ancient record to indicate that they did so. The suggestion that these dates coincided with any known event in the life of Rameses II—including his date of accession to the throne or his birthday—is illusionary, and seems to have originated only when the temples were relocated in the 1960s.

Nonetheless, Rameses II sits here comfortably among the other gods.

In fact, all ancient Egyptian pharaohs became gods when they died. As the Pyramid Texts (religious texts dating back to at least 2400–2300 BC) put it, "He [the dead king] is a god, older than the oldest. He is served by thousands and receives offerings from hundreds." Indeed, part of the living king's authority lay in his fictional lineage to all (or most) of the god-kings of the past—illustrated beautifully in the case of Sethy I (Rameses II's father) and Rameses II by the king lists to be found on the temple walls at Abydos.

Quite early on in Egyptian history, cults also developed around the living king, but—while recognizing that the living king was regarded as having divine attributes—there is considerable debate concerning whether the king was regarded as truly divine, truly human, or both, even in those historical periods for which we have a good body of textual evidence.

The argument that the living king was considered divine is bolstered by the depiction of the king on the same scale as the gods, and far larger than his subjects, and the frequent use of the word *netjer* or 'divine being' in association with his image. After his accession to the throne, in any case, the king was certainly regarded as the son of Re and the living image of Horus.

Alternatively, these elements could simply have been hyperbole, and unquestionably the king was regarded in ancient Egypt as subservient to the gods, particularly with regard to temple ritual. Unlike the gods, he was certainly not regarded as omniscient or invulnerable, nor could he perform miracles.

As always, the reality of the perceived divinity of the king probably lay somewhere in between—he was simultaneously human and divine. Such an idea would not run counter to Egyptian theological thinking, which contained many such paradoxes.

The sunrise from the rear of the Great Temple sanctuary.

Quite often in the Great Temple, the human Rameses II is depicted as making offerings to his divine self, or the deified Rameses II has been inserted at a later date into a relief containing gods and goddesses, and it is thought that very occasionally in ancient Egyptian history a king was declared *fully* divine in his own lifetime. This process does not seem to have happened by royal decree but was 'earned' through a king's length of reign or some other measure of success.

In the case of Amenhotep III, at the time of his thirtieth year of ruling the country, the king declared himself to be a god. After this time, there are representations of the king making offerings to himself as a god, and he is portrayed with the horns of Amun (as Rameses is here) and the curved beard of the gods. It is unclear, though, whether this newly acquired divine status was a permanent characteristic, or something only associated with certain festivals.

Rameses II is unquestionably equal to the other gods in the sanctuary of the Great Temple, and it seems certain that his divine status also surpasses that normally associated with a living ruler. How that degree of divinity might have been perceived as measuring up to that of his dead predecessors is unknown, and it may be that the perceived level of his divinity was greater here in the far-flung territory of Nubia than it was in Egypt.

The Small Temple

The hill into which the Small Temple was carved, 100 meters (330 feet) away from the Great Temple, had a pre-existing association with the goddess Hathor of Abshek (a local form of an ancient goddess of many attributes, but fundamentally of femininity).

It is reasonable to assume that the Small Temple was carved out of the second hill at the same time as the Great Temple was carved out of the first. Certainly, it was carved relatively early in Rameses' reign, as it is also dedicated to Queen Nefertiry, his first (co-)Great Wife (with Queen Isetneferet), and mother of his first male heir.

As noted earlier, this was not the first time a Nubian temple had been dedicated to a great royal wife. Amenhotep III had similarly dedicated a temple to his wife Tiye—around 150 years earlier—at Sedeinga, 240 kilometers (150 miles) to the south. However, such dual dedications of temples were rare in ancient Egyptian history.

The Small Temple is completely rock-cut, extending 24 meters (79 feet) into the mountain. The rock here may not have been of the same quality as that from which the Great Temple was carved, as a number of slight adjustments in alignment were evidently made while construction was underway—between the façade and the hall, and the hall and the vestibule, for example.

Both temples share the same general characteristics, and the rooms the same functions, but the Small Temple has only one pillared hall, not two. Behind this lies a vestibule, with two small associated storerooms, and the sanctuary.

As visitors approached the Small Temple they would first see the colossal statues of Rameses II and Nefertiry that are cut to a variety of depths in the façade.

Façade of the Small Temple, Abu Simbel.

Standing 10 meters (33 feet) high, only two of the six statues are of Nefertiry, but, unusually, these are of approximately the same height as those of the king, perhaps indicating the esteem in which she was held. Four sons and two daughters of Nefertiry are depicted by the legs of Rameses II and the Queen. To the north of the entrance, and from left to right, these are Princes Meryatum and Meryre; Princesses Meryetamun and Henttawy; and, finally, Princes Amenhirwenemef and Prehirwenemef. To the south of the entrance, the same royal children appear, but in reverse order. So, as at the Great Temple, the façade is a monument to the royal family, in this case specifically to Rameses, Nefertiry, and their offspring.

Rameses II wearing the *atef* crown associated with the god Osiris (Small Temple façade).

Queen Nefertiry (Small Temple façade).

The pillared hall of the Small Temple. The god Thoth appears on the second column on the left, and Rameses II offers incense on the column to the right. Further to the rear on the left, the seated goddess Hathor of Abshek is presented with flowers, and, to the rear on the right, the goddess Mut can be seen in a similar scene.

Opposite: Rameses II crowned by Horus of Maha and Seth of Nubet: left side of the southwest wall of the pillared hall.

Hathor pillar, the pillared hall of the Small Temple.

Queen Nefertiry holds the ritual rattle (sistrum ♀) associated with the goddess Hathor and wears the Hathor headdress of cow horns, surmounted by a sun disk and two plumes. The king wears several crowns including—on the northern or right-hand statue—the *atef* crown (⚜) that combines the *hedjet*, the crown generally associated with Upper Egypt (⚐), with an ostrich feather on each side—

representing truth, justice, morality, and balance—and associated with the cult of the god Osiris.

As at the Great Temple, but in a horizontal line above the statues, the statues of the king are individually named: 'Sun of the Rulers,' 'The Ruler of the Two Lands,' 'The Beloved of Amun,' and 'The Beloved of Atum.' They may also have served as points of communication between worshippers and the gods.

Nefertiry holds the sistrum rattle associated with the goddess Hathor and offers flowers to the Nile goddess Anukis: middle of the southwest wall of the pillared hall.

Hathor columns of the pillared hall. Through the pillars (with manifestations of Horus), Rameses offers wine to Re-Horakhty; the ram-headed god Heryshef: northeast wall of the pillared hall.

The king and queen offer flowers to the goddess Taweret: left of the central doorway in the vestibule.

An inscription on the buttresses between the statues states that Rameses II intended

A sanctuary of great and mighty monuments for the great royal wife Nefertiry, beloved of Mut, for whom the sun god Re shines. . . . He [the king] has had a sanctuary of everlasting craftsmanship excavated in the mountain in Nubia, which the King of Upper and Lower Egypt, Usermaatre-Setpenre, has made for the great royal wife Nefertiry, beloved of Mut, in Nubia, like Re, for ever and ever.

The intention may have been to carve the rock projecting above the entrance into a statue of Hathor, but this was not carried out.

Passing through the entrance, a visitor would enter into a remarkable structure that was wholly designed for its purpose as a temple to the goddess of femininity, and to Nefertiry.

Certainly on the southeast wall there are the traditional smiting scenes—Rameses, accompanied by the queen, kills a Nubian to the right of the door, and kills an 'Asiatic' to the left—in his role in maintaining order and stability in Egypt—but the unusually elongated figures of the goddesses and of the queen, and the presentation of flowers to the gods, immediately project a gentler aspect in comparison to the decoration of the Great Temple, even though the color scheme of predominately bright red, yellow, and black would have been the same.

Through the entrance where the king offers flowers to Hathor of Abshek (to the left) and the queen offers flowers to Isis (to the right), the priests would have entered the pillared hall dominated by two sets of three pillars topped along the central aisle by a beautiful representation of the face of Hathor within the handle and sounding box of the sistrum rattle associated with her worship. The other three sides of these columns are covered by representations of the king, the queen, and gods, displaying great subtlety and, often, delicacy.

The southwest (left) wall reliefs begin from the left with a representation of Rameses II being crowned by Horus of Maha, with the head of a falcon, and Seth of Nubet, with the head of an imaginary animal. Unusually, Seth is portrayed here as a god who protects the pharaoh and gives him power over foreign lands rather than as the god associated with chaos.

The family of Rameses II came from the eastern Nile Delta, where Seth had developed as the patron deity through a complex route that appears to have involved the combination of the Egyptian god Seth with the sky gods of northern Syria brought to Egypt by the Hyksos—an enigmatic group of people from the eastern Mediterranean who ruled Egypt from the eastern Delta between about 1640 and 1530 BC. Indeed, Rameses's father, Sethy ('the one of Seth'), was named for the god.

To the right of this scene Nefertiry offers the sistrum rattle of Hathor and flowers to the goddess Anukis, who originated in Nubia as a personification

Opposite: Hathor, in the form of a cow, emerges from the rock face, while Rameses (to the left) offers her flowers: sanctuary, Small Temple.

Nefertiry is crowned by Hathor of Abshek (in front) and Isis (behind) in a scene to the right of the central doorway in the vestibule.

of the Nile (her headdress is made of reeds) and was one of a triad of gods associated with Elephantine Island (Aswan) alongside the god Khnum and the goddess Satis. To the right again, Rameses II offers Maat to Amun-Re in a now familiar ritual scene of the king's role in maintaining order in the face of chaos.

Along the northeast (right) wall, from right to left, Rameses II presents offerings to Ptah (who sits within a shrine); then the king offers flowers to the ancient ram-headed fertility god Heryshef, who had his cult center at Hnes (near modern Beni Suef in Middle Egypt), where Rameses II greatly extended the god's principal temple. To the left again, Nefertiry makes offerings to Hathor of Dendera, and, finally, the king offers wine to Re-Horakhty.

The three entrances to the vestibule form two pillars. On the left-hand pillar the queen presents flowers and holds a sistrum before Hathor of Abshek to whom the temple is dedicated, and on the right-hand pillar, the queen offers flowers to Mut.

Passing through the middle doorway, the priests would enter the vestibule, which would presumably have seen offering rituals similar to those that occurred in the Great Temple. Two small storerooms lie to the left and right of the vestibule. Above the storeroom to the left, Nefertiry offers flowers to the goddess Hathor in the form of a cow standing on a boat; to the right, Rameses offers flowers in a similar scene.

Elsewhere in the vestibule, offerings are made by the king to different localized forms of the god Horus—Horus of Miam (the Nubian town of Aniba to the north), of Baki (the fortress at Quban, near the original location of the temple of Dakka, also to the north), and of Buhen (a fortress near moden Wadi Halfa)—all to the left of the sanctuary door. He also makes an offering to Amun-Re in the same place. To the right of the sanctuary door, the king makes an offering to Re-Horakhty, and the queen to Khnum, Satis, and Anukis, the triad of Elephantine.

Looking back from the sanctuary door toward the temple entrance, the priests would face two remarkable scenes. To the left, the king and queen offer flowers to the goddess Taweret, the goddess protector of pregnant women and those giving birth, not in her usual form of a hippopotamus, but as a woman wearing a Hathor headdress.

To the right, the priests would face one of the most elegant images ever created in ancient Egypt. The graceful form of Nefertiry, wearing a Nubian wig, is 'crowned' by the equally graceful forms of the goddesses Hathor of Abshek (in front of the queen) and Isis (behind the queen). All three wear the uraeus (a stylized rearing cobra), flat-topped cylindrical headdress or crown (modius), solar disk, and cow horns (with the addition of twin plumes in the case of Nefertiry).

Intriguingly, all three carry the ankh, the sign of life (), which was normally carried only by gods in temple scenes. This may suggest that Nefertiry was regarded as having a greater than usual divine status for a queen during her lifetime, probably through association with the divine Rameses II. Perhaps this process of becoming truly divine in her own right was cut short by the death of Nefertiry a few years before the thirtieth anniversary of Rameses' ascension to the throne of Egypt.

This representation in the Small Temple, and others where the queen makes an offering to the gods on her own, suggest that the ritual activities in this temple might have been significantly different from those conducted in the Great Temple. The known roles of the queens of Egypt in temple ritual suggest that some queens may have played a greater role alongside their husbands than others, and that the title 'god's wife' was even used selectively, particularly from the New Kingdom onward, though the ritual aspect of this title is unclear. Thus, it is possible that when the sanctuary doors of the Small Temple were opened, the queen may have been involved in the most sacred rites.

These possibilities are amplified by the decoration of the sanctuary itself. On the left wall, the queen offers incense and carries a sistrum before Mut and Hathor. On the right wall, the king offers incense and pours a libation before his deified self and Nefertiry.

In the center of the sanctuary, Hathor, in the form of a cow, is carved as if emerging from the hill (slightly to the right of center, possibly because of weaknesses found in the rock) with a figure of the king under her chin and a Hathor sistrum on either side.

Finally, to the left of the Hathor statue, Rameses is shown offering her flowers.

So, whatever the arguments might be concerning the divine or mortal status of Nefertiry, there is no doubt that Rameses had the last word.

Rameses II kneels before Re-Horakhty while Thoth writes on the leaves of a sacred tree.

3 | Gods and Goddesses

Approximately 1,500 ancient Egyptian gods and goddesses are known by name, though a much smaller number are known in any detail. Broadly, these divine beings—who influenced the lives of all Egyptians, from the lowest to the highest ranks—might be categorized as being in 'human,' 'animal,' 'human-animal,' or other 'composite' forms.

Cosmic deities and those associated with the heavens and earth—who were worshipped from the earliest periods of Egyptian society—are usually represented as human in form. Other gods, such as the ancient fertility god Min and deified pharaohs, also appear as recognizably human.

Other deities were represented in animal form, such as gods represented as a falcon, a bull, a ram, or a lion; or goddesses represented as a cow, a lioness, a snake, or a vulture. Again, some of these representations stretch back to the earliest days of Egypt.

Half-human/half-animal deities might have the head of an animal and the body of a human or vice versa. The Great Sphinx at Giza is the most famous example, and one of the most ancient. The essential form of the god or goddess is usually determined by the head. In this way, what we most often think of as a sphinx is a 'human' deity who has taken on the body of a lion, while the goddess Sekhmet is a lioness who has taken on the body of a woman.

Composite deities can combine different human and animal deities (or their characteristics)—sometimes, many of them. They may combine an assortment of human and animal parts; this is the world of the hawk-baboon and the ram-headed scarab beetle.

Very few gods had a single standard representation. Thoth, for example, might appear in human form, as an ibis, or as a baboon. Amun might appear as a human, a ram, or a goose. Hathor might appear as a human, a cow, a woman with the head of a cow, or a woman with a face combining human and cow-like features.

This variability reflects the understanding that the image of a god or goddess was not intended to be a true likeness of the deity. They were formal representations of aspects of divine beings who were otherwise described as 'hidden,' 'mysterious,' or 'unknown,' and simply intended as a physical focus of worship for individuals or priests.

While some gods were viewed as essentially helpful—Thoth, Horus, and Isis, for example, were venerated for their healing powers—most gods were regarded as essentially hostile and in need of placation. The nature of some—often goddesses—could simply be ambivalent. Hathor was indeed the goddess of love and the celebration of music, but she could also appear as a goddess of destruction.

The ancient Egyptian deities were often remarkably human in their changing moods.

While the concept of around 1,500 deities may be alarming, many of these were the same god or goddess called by a different name, associated with a particular location, or representing a particular characteristic of the deity. We have already meet Horus *of Maha* and Hathor *of Abshek* in the context of the Abu Simbel temples, for example.

Many of the others on the list were minor household divinities or demons associated with the day-to-day worship of ordinary people. Few of these were ever to be seen in the context of the great temples. Only the gods who stood at the very center of ancient Egyptian theology—ancient gods, great gods, and those responsible for the creation and the maintenance of the cosmos—were represented on those walls, though even this representation was subject to variation across the country and over time.

As the centuries passed, the major deities were often organized into 'father,' 'mother,' and 'son' (or, occasionally, 'daughter') groupings known as triads. The best-known of these today is the triad of Osiris, Isis, and Horus with its cult center at Abydos, but the triads of Ptah, Sekhmet, and Nefertem (Memphis), and Amun, Mut, and Khonsu (Thebes) were equally familiar to the ancient Egyptians. The Elephantine Triad of Khnum, Satis, and Anukis held particular sway over the southern borders of Egypt and into Nubia.

Over time again, many individual gods and goddesses gradually lost their significance or were absorbed or linked into aspects of the major deities to create composite gods such as Re-Horakhty, Amun-Re, and Atum-Khepri (representing the morning and evening manifestations of the sun). This process of creating composite gods could ultimately draw in multiple deities (as in the form of Hormakhet-Khepri-Re-Atum, which combined normally separate aspects of the sun god) who individually had shared similar characteristics.

Most of the great deities and some of the interesting lesser regional deities are to be found in both of the temples at Abu Simbel, with a small number only found in one or the other. The following alphabetical list introduces the main characteristics of the deities discussed in this brief guide to the temples.

Amun/Amun-Re

Amun/Amun-Re

Amun-Re is usually portrayed in human form wearing a short kilt (sometimes with a bull's tail attached), a feather-patterned tunic, and a double-plumed crown. He can be found with red or blue skin, and is often shown striding out, or, as 'king of the gods,' seated on a throne.

An important local god from around 2100 BC, Amun gradually displaced the god Montu (the falcon-headed god of war) at Thebes over the next 150 years. By the time the temples at Abu Simbel were constructed, however, Amun, as Amun-Re, was considered to be the supreme god. The goddess Mut was his consort, and the lunar god Khonsu their son.

Despite the variety of forms of representation of Amun-Re, he was regarded as having an imperceptible nature—'invisible,' 'concealed,' or 'mysterious of form.'

More than a century before the temples at Abu Simbel were built, Karnak was said to contain the 'mound of the beginning' where Amun had brought the world into existence. He was also credited with creating the whole universe through his thoughts.

From about 1950 BC, Amun-Re was referred to at Karnak as 'king of the gods' and 'lord of the thrones of the two lands' (Upper and Lower Egypt).

Borrowing attributes from his Theban colleague, the war god Montu, Amun was a warrior god as well. When the Hyksos were finally expelled from Egypt around 1550 BC, it was Amun who received the credit. He also protected the pharaoh in battle. It was to Amun that Rameses II called in the heat of battle at Qadesh—to the 'lord of victory,' the 'lover of strength'—and it was to Karnak Temple ('the most select of places') and Amun that the spoils of victory were brought.

Representations of Amun-Re can be found over 40 times throughout the temples at Abu Simbel—from the stelae on either side of the ramp leading to the terrace, to the statues of the gods in the sanctuary of the Great Temple. As a general guide, representations of Amun-Re tend to be on the left (or south) side of the temple, those of Re-Horakhty on the right.

Anukis

Anukis

Anukis appears as a woman wearing a low crown from which extend bound plumes or reeds (sometimes also with ribbons to the rear of the crown or a rearing cobra [uraeus] at the front). As well as an ankh, representing her divinity, she may carry a papyrus scepter.

The goddess was associated with the southern borders of Egypt, particularly with the area around Aswan. She was originally considered to be a daughter of Re but became associated with Elephantine Island as the daughter of Khnum and his consort Satis.

Anukis was a popular goddess and was regarded as having a maternal role toward the king—she was sometimes referred to specifically as 'the mother of the king.'

Atum

The god Atum represented the evening form of the sun god, and usually appears in temple decoration in human form wearing the dual crown of Upper and Lower Egypt. Particularly when he is associated with the underworld, he may appear with a ram's head or as an old man.

Like other aspects of the sun, Atum's ancient cult had been particularly associated with Heliopolis, but, over time, Re came to predominate there—though Atum remained important as 'Lord of Heliopolis.'

He was regarded as a self-created deity from whom the first gods were derived through his semen (or his saliva). He was the father of the gods and, by eventual extension, the king.

Hathor

One of the oldest and most important goddesses, Hathor is usually represented as a woman wearing a long wig bound by a band or ribbon, or she may wear a vulture-shaped cap topped with a narrow cylindrical crown *(modius)*, and a sun disk between curved cow horns.

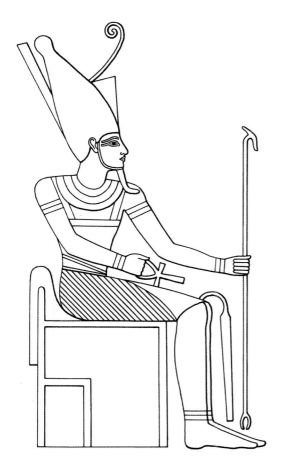

Atum

Ha/Horus Ha

Ha was a god of the desert. He is normally depicted in human form, with the hieroglyph of three hills that denotes 'desert' or 'foreign lands' on his head (⌣⌣).

He was closely associated with the Western Desert and oases, providing protection against nomadic peoples and Libyan tribesmen.

Hathor and Nefertiry

In later depictions, Hathor, as the 'generic' female deity, becomes difficult to distinguish from other goddesses, especially Isis, as seen in the vestibule of the Small Temple. In such cases, only the associated text allows one to be sure which goddess is depicted. Hathor is often dressed in a red or turquoise (or both) sheath dress.

Rarely for a goddess, she sometimes carries the *was* power scepter (a staff with a stylized animal head at the top and a fork at the bottom), or a papyrus reed stem, or, often, a musical rattle (sistrum).

Worship of Hathor probably dates back to the earliest period of the Egyptian state, if not beyond. She was an immensely popular goddess and many everyday objects carry a depiction of her. Her roles included those of goddess of sexuality and fertility, among her numerous other attributes.

As was true of so many gods and goddesses, Hathor was closely associated with Re (she wears his sun disk). She was his wife or daughter, which accounts for her rapid growth in importance from the earliest period in Egyptian history. As 'The Golden One' she accompanied the sun god on his daily travel on the solar boat, and, by extension, assisted the reigning king in his daily rebirth with the sun. By contrast, she was also Re's vengeful 'Eye' who was capable of destroying humanity in her anger.

In her cow form, she also protected the king and acted as his nurse; she was often depicted as breastfeeding him. In this and other aspects, Hathor was the mother of the king and he the 'son of Hathor,' which combined well with the role of the king as the living incarnation of Horus. Importantly, Hathor was also the 'wife' of the king, and hence, as at Abu Simbel, the king's Great Wife is seen acting as her priestess, and as a human manifestation of the goddess.

Hathor was the 'beautiful one' and was inseparably associated with femininity. She was believed to aid women in conception, labor, and childbirth.

Heryshef

The god Heryshef (Arsaphes) normally appears as a long-horned ram or a man with a ram's head. In the latter form, he is seen striding forward like a king and wearing a royal kilt. As he was associated with Osiris and Re, he often wears the complex *atef* crown (🦃) complete with ostrich feathers (as Rameses II does outside the Small Temple on the far right of the façade), or the disk of the sun god.

Heryshef was another ancient god, whose cult center was at Ihnasiya (Hnes or Herakleopolis Magna, close to Beni Suef in the middle of Egypt). His temple there was greatly enlarged by Rameses II.

Heryshef may have been a creator god—his name means 'he who is upon his lake,' perhaps suggesting a connection with the primeval waters, or this may simply be an association with his sacred lake at Hnes.

He was most closely associated with Osiris and Re as part of the soul of these gods, which defined strength and power and could move between the human and divine planes. The word for this component of the soul, *ba*, sounded the same as the ancient Egyptian word for ram.

Horus

Horus

A number of distinct deities bore the name 'Horus' in ancient Egypt, and they are not always easy to distinguish from each other. However, the most prominent 'Horus' was the patron deity of the Egyptian monarchy. As such, he was originally depicted as a perching falcon shown in profile but with the tail feathers turned so that they could be seen fully. Later, he was most often depicted as a human figure with the head of a falcon and wearing the double crown of Egypt (⚕) signifying his power over the whole country.

Over time, the forms of Horus merged with other gods and their characteristics, making distinctions even more problematic.

There is reasonable evidence that the worship of the principal form of Horus predates the formation of the Egyptian state, and temples associated with the god can be found from an early date throughout the country, from the Delta to the far south. In the south of Egypt, he can be found with Hathor as his consort, and with Harsomptus ('Horus the Uniter') as his son in the later (Ptolemaic) temples at Edfu and Kom Ombo.

Within Nubia itself, there are a number of temples dedicated to local forms of the god—Horus of Baki at Quban, Horus of Buhen, Horus of Miam at Aniba, and, of course, Horus of Maha at Abu Simbel.

Horus deities were popular in ancient Egypt and are often found depicted on amulets, or on plaques seeking to utilize his power for healing.

The Egyptian word *hir*, from which the god derives his name, means 'the one on high' or 'the distant one,' referring to the soaring flight of the falcon. In this aspect as a sky god, Horus was 'lord of the sky'—his right eye was the sun, and his left eye the moon. His speckled breast contained the stars, and the sky lay between his wings, whose beating produced the wind. Horus was also worshipped as 'god of the east,' the direction of the sunrise.

Horus became the son of Osiris and Isis, possibly combining with another earlier deity in this 'family' to become a divine infant.

As the son of Isis and Osiris, and in his broader theological context, Horus was intimately associated with the king. Indeed, due to his parentage, he was the mythical heir—'Lord of the Two Lands'—to the throne of Egypt. From the earliest times, the pharaoh's Horus name was written in a rectangular shape (known as a *serekh*) that depicted Horus as a falcon perched on a palace enclosure. This seems to have represented the role of the king as a mediator between humans and the gods, or the god-like properties of the king himself.

Isis

The origins of the goddess Isis are not clear, but she came to eclipse all the other gods and goddesses of ancient Egypt.

Isis (Iset in Egyptian) was usually represented as a woman in a long sheath dress, crowned with the hieroglyph for 'throne' (𓊨 '*set*'), which represents her name, or with the horns and sun disk that she acquired from Hathor. She may also carry the rattle (sistrum) and beaded necklace associated with Hathor, but often, more simply, she may only carry the ankh sign and a papyrus staff, as other goddesses do. Most often she is depicted standing, but she may also be found kneeling, or in the pose of mourning, with one hand lifted to her face.

Her arms may be outstretched around the figure of Osiris, and her arms may be winged.

Isis

For most of Egyptian history, Isis was worshipped in association with other gods rather than individually—particularly with Osiris and Horus. The sole worship of Isis, as at Philae, appears to have been a relatively late phenomenon as she absorbed the characteristics of many other goddesses.

Yet the influence of her cult became very widespread throughout the Greco-Roman world—in Athens, in Rome, and in the far-flung provinces—rivaling the major cults of the Mediterranean and beyond. Her cult was popular, personal, and very strong—worship of Isis continued at Philae into the sixth century AD, long after the rest of the Roman world had been declared Christian.

Isis and Osiris were the children of Geb (earth) and Nut (sky). Isis married Osiris and assisted him during his mythical rule of Egypt. Osiris was murdered and dismembered by his brother Seth, but with the help of her sister Nephthys, Isis discovered the scattered parts of her husband's body, reunited them, became pregnant, and gave birth to their child Horus.

The image of Isis nursing Horus on her lap was immensely popular in ancient Egypt, as were the tales of her steadfast care of her son when danger threatened—magically healing him whenever necessary. Indeed, Isis protected and nurtured her son until he was able to avenge his father's murder and inherit the kingship of Egypt.

In this manner, Isis also became the symbolic mother of the pharaoh, who was the living incarnation of her son Horus. Further, as her name was written using the hieroglyph for 'throne' or 'seat,' Isis also represented a general sense of the power of the king.

Her magical powers—which had revived the dead Osiris—were a vital aspect of her persona, and her name was invoked for protection and healing, particularly with regard to children. Her magical powers and knowledge were the greatest among all the gods.

Alongside her sister Nephthys, and because of her actions after the murder of Osiris, Isis was considered to be the archetypal mourner, sustainer, and protector of the dead—caring for the recently deceased in a personal way as would a devoted mother.

Iusaas

Iusaas (perhaps meaning 'she comes who is great') usually appears in the form of a woman with a scarab beetle on her head.

She was associated with Heliopolis, but seldom elsewhere, and seems to have been a female counterpart to the god Atum, as well as possessing a more general aspect embodying the female creative powers.

Kamutef

Kamutef was a fertility god—a local manifestation at Thebes of the god Min whose cult center was at Koptos, 35 kilometers (22 miles) to the north. His name means 'bull of his mother'—meaning he was regarded as fathering himself—an epithet that was also used for Min. The implication was that he represented an endless cycle of rebirth and renewal.

Over time, Kamutef appears to have become more of a concept than an independent deity. He was incorporated as Amun-Kamutef (emphasizing the fertility aspect of the god Amun) or, as at Abu Simbel, as Min-Amun-Kamutef.

Khepri

The god Khepri, the morning form of the sun god, is usually represented as a scarab beetle (🪲) with varying degrees of stylization. In this form, he is often colored blue—either in paint or in lapis lazuli—representing his association with the heavens, though he appears in a more realistic black in papyrus texts. He may also be seen pushing a sun disk ahead of him. The scarab may occasionally be combined with other animals such as a falcon or vulture.

Khepri could also be depicted as a human with a scarab head. He is seen in this form in Queen Nefertiry's tomb in the Valley of the Queens.

He sometimes wears the *atef* crown of Osiris to demonstrate the joining of the heavens and the underworld. He may also appear as a scarab with a ram's head—as Atum-Khepri—representing the rising and setting suns.

It seems that Khepri was seldom worshipped on his own—though the colossal statue of the scarab god beside the sacred lake at Karnak temple, and the ubiquitous presence of scarab amulets and seals, speak to the scarab's ever-present role as a symbol of creation and resurrection.

Khepri represented the solar disk rising in the eastern sky, as part of its three aspects: 'Khepri in the morning, Re-Horakhty at midday, and Atum in the evening.' He was the god of the first sunrise at the moment of creation, and thus closely associated with Atum as Atum-Khepri.

His original role may have been simpler—the ancient Egyptians seeing the parallel between the beetle's behavior of rolling a mud or dung ball with its rear legs and the emergence of the scarab's young from the mud base, and the god pushing the solar disk (with his front legs) across the sky on its daily route.

Khnum

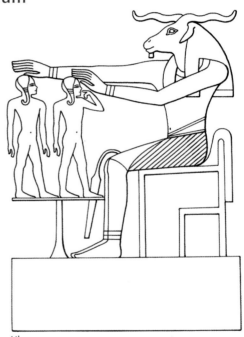

Khnum

Khnum was associated with the Nile River and the creation of life. He usually appears as a man with a ram's head, a short kilt, and a long three-stranded wig. Originally, he was depicted with horizontal undulating sheep's horns, but later he is seen with short curved ram's horns, or sometimes both. He may also wear two tall feathers, the White Crown of Upper Egypt, or the *atef* crown.

Khnum was most closely associated with Elephantine Island in Aswan and was said to control the Nile's annual flood from caves below the river. Here, he was head of a triad of deities that included the goddesses Satis and Anukis.

His association with the regenerative powers of the river probably accounts for one of the most evocative representations among the ancient Egyptian gods—Khnum sitting at his potter's wheel shaping humans and all other living things.

He was also 'lord of the crocodiles,' through an association with the goddess Neith (a very ancient and important 'creator' goddess celebrated particularly in Lower Egypt) who was regarded as the mother of the chief crocodile god Sobek.

Khonsu

Khonsu was a moon god whose character changed greatly over time.

He normally appears in the form of a young man tightly wrapped in a close-fitting garment. His arms, however, are usually partially or completely free. He often wears a full moon disk resting on a new moon on his head, and, as the 'son' of Amun and Mut, he sometimes has a sidelock of hair that was characteristic of boyhood in ancient Egypt (though he may simultaneously wear the curved beard of a god).

He may hold the crook and flail associated with Osiris and Horus, together with a *was* (𓌀) or *djed*-headed (𓊽) staff. Characteristically, he wears a heavy necklace back and front, with a crescent form at the chest.

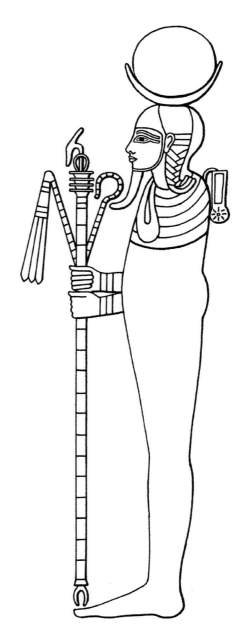

Khonsu

He may also appear as a falcon-headed human, distinguishable from Horus and Re by the presence of a lunar disk and crescent moon. As a moon god, he may also appear occasionally as a baboon.

A number of temples dedicated to Khonsu were built in Egypt, the most important one being erected within the precinct of Amun at Karnak sometime after the reign of Rameses II.

As a member of the Theban 'family' of Amun, Mut, and Khonsu ('Khonsu of Thebes'), he appeared in the form of a healer, or as 'Khonsu the child' or 'Khonsu the provider.' Through his participation in the reckoning of time, particularly gestation, he was known as 'Khonsu the decider of life and its span.'

Later, and not very far from Thebes, at Kom Ombo temple, Khonsu came to be regarded as the son of Sobek and Hathor, and at Edfu he was associated with Osiris. He was also linked to Shu (the god of air) and Horus.

Maat

The goddess Maat represented truth, justice, and order in the cosmos.

Almost without exception, Maat appears in human form wearing an ostrich feather on her head. However, the feather itself may also represent the goddess. Her arms may be winged.

A small temple to Maat was built in the grounds of the temple to Montu at Karnak, but she usually appears in the context of temples to other gods.

The presentation of Maat—in small statue form— to the gods (particularly to Amun, Re, Ptah, and to Maat's own consort, Thoth), was a central component of the king's ritual activity in temples. In this manner, the king offered his own effort in maintaining order and justice on the god's behalf.

Maat was a 'daughter of Re' and was also associated with Osiris ('the lord of *maat*') early in the history of the Egyptian state. This may explain why some of the characteristics of Maat were absorbed by Isis later in Egypt's history.

As a daughter of Re, Maat was also considered to be the reigning king's 'sister,' and both the legitimacy of the king and the judgment of his reign were assessed by his perceived ability to uphold *maat*.

Maat

Maat represented order and balance in the universe, which had been established at the creation (this was the basis of her relationship to Re). That order, however, had to be constantly maintained and renewed—not least by the king. Through her relationship with order and balance, Maat was inevitably drawn also into the concept of justice.

All ancient Egyptians were expected to live within the principles of *maat*, and upon death, it was against the feather of Maat that the deceased's heart would be weighed on the scales of judgment.

Merymutef

Somewhat more obscure than many of the deities to be seen at Abu Simbel, Merymutef ('Beloved of his mother') was known as the 'Lord of Khayet' (Manqabad, on the west bank of the Nile about 12 kilometers [8 miles] north of Asyut) and for much of his known history was tied only to that place.

Merymutef appears as a ram-headed young god with both horizontal and curved horns, holding the *was* scepter and an ankh. He may also appear in fully human form, or with the head of a falcon.

As at Abu Simbel, Merymutef was sometimes associated with the equally obscure goddess Ipt (or Ipipt or Ipui), 'lady of the sky, mistress of the Two Lands'—possibly a local form of Hathor. She appears as a lioness-headed woman, wearing a sun disk, and holding a papyrus flower staff and ankh.

Merymutef was also connected to the goddess Nut (goddess of the sky) and it has been suggested that Merymutef was regarded as the son of Nut and Geb—at least locally—alongside his older 'brother' Horwer ('Horus the Elder').

As time progressed, Merymutef, or his name, appeared elsewhere directly associated with Hathor—in a turquoise mine in southwest Sinai; in the temple of Rameses's father, Sethy I, at Abydos; and at Karnak temple.

Min

As the god of male sexual powers, Min had a long and illustrious career. He usually appears in human form with an erect penis. His body is tightly wrapped, except for his left hand, which holds his penis, and his right arm, which is raised in a protective or smiting manner of unknown meaning.

He wears a cap or crown with ribbons attached to it and two tall plumes. He may also carry a flail and wear a collar. His skin is always black, perhaps as an association with the fertile soil of Egypt. He is often seen with the cos-type lettuce in offering scenes, as the plant was believed to have aphrodisiac qualities.

Min was most closely associated with the city of Gebtu (or Koptos—modern Qift, between Luxor and Qena), though he was worshipped throughout Egypt. His main festival, 'the coming forth of Min,' coincided with the harvest.

By the time the temples at Abu Simbel were created, Min was most closely associated with Amun at Thebes, becoming the manifestation of Amun as a primeval creator god. As Amun-Min, he became an important component of the coronation and jubilee celebrations of the pharaoh, representing the king's potency.

Min

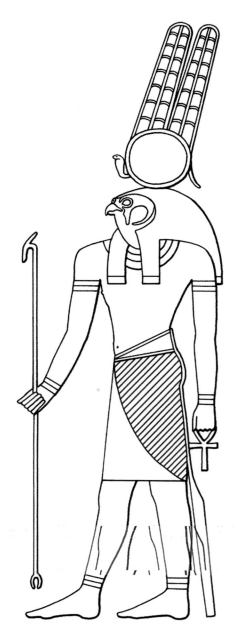

Montu

Montu, the war god, was worshipped particularly within the region around Thebes. He is normally depicted as a human with a falcon's head, though he may also be seen in earlier representations as a falcon.

Sometimes he carries the curved *khepesh* sword (⤼), familiar from smiting scenes, in keeping with

Montu

his warlike aspect. He usually wears the sun disk and uraeus (stylized rearing cobra head) and two plumes (which help distinguish him from Re and other falcon gods).

His consorts were the solar goddess Raettawy and an obscure local goddess Tjenenyet, a goddess of beer brewing, but known particularly in her role as Montu's consort in the town of Armant 20 kilometers (12 miles) south of Thebes.

The god's four main centers of worship were all in the area around Thebes, including at Karnak, where he had his own temple to the north of the great temple dedicated to Amun.

Montu's fortunes essentially rose with those of his hometown. Four Theban rulers of the Eleventh Dynasty (approximately 2080–1940 BC) bore the name Montuhotep ('Montu is content'), and the god gradually assumed an individual importance throughout Egypt.

Montu was also sometimes characterized as a southern counterpart to Re, combining as Mont-Re, though his importance began to diminish as that of Amun increased. Nonetheless, he remained popular with warrior pharaohs.

Mut

Originally a lioness-headed goddess, over time Mut most often appeared in fully human form in a long dress colored red or blue, sometimes with a pattern resembling feathers.

She may wear a vulture headdress, topped by the White Crown of Egypt, or the double crown of the Two Lands—the only goddess to do so. She may sit on a throne or stand holding a papyrus or lily-headed staff. In her lioness-headed form, she is closely linked at Karnak Temple with the goddess Sekhmet.

Mut was the wife of Amun and the mother of Khonsu—whom she may often be found nursing. In her role as the consort of Amun, she replaced an earlier goddess named Amaunet. In general, the trio of gods, Amun, Mut, and Khonsu, appear as much more of a 'family' than many other divine triads. Within this structure, Mut is the mature mother figure and the undisputed queen of the gods. She was also known to have an oracle to whom the faithful could bring their most intractable problems as a child might come to a mother.

The worship of Mut probably started in Upper Egypt, although she had sanctuaries in Heliopolis, Giza, and Tanis in the Delta. She appears on almost every wall in the temple of Amun at Karnak, but still maintained her own temple to the south of that temple—much of it constructed by Amenhotep III. This temple also contained many statues of Sekhmet, the northern lioness goddess. Mut was carried in her own sacred barque during the many great festival processions associated with Amun.

Unsurprisingly, Mut was closely associated with the queens of Egypt, who would wear the vulture headdress as a symbol of their relationship.

In her lioness aspect, she was an 'Eye of Re' alongside Sekhmet and Tefnut, and she was also closely associated with Ptah in Memphis.

The goddess Mut (center) tenderly embraces Rameses II on the east (front) side of the second column on the left in the small pillared hall.

Osiris

One of the most important figures in the Egyptian pantheon, Osiris was the god of death, resurrection, and fertility.

He is usually portrayed in human form with a tight sheath around his body, in the same way as Ptah and Min. His skin may be black or green, both colors associated with fertility: the silt deposited by the Nile flood, and the green shoots of new growth (rebirth) that came forth from it.

He sits or stands upright with his legs within the sheath, but his arms are free and he holds the crook

Osiris

and flail of a king. Often, and throughout Egyptian history, he wears the White Crown of Upper Egypt or the later, more complex *atef* crown ()—a similar crown, with added side feathers, sometimes with horizontal horns and solar disks. He may also wear a broad collar and bracelet.

Osiris was closely associated with the *djed* pillar (), meaning 'stability'—a segmented pillar that may represent the tree in which Osiris's body was trapped, or the god's spine.

Most often he is seated on a throne, with Isis and her sister Nephthys (and occasionally Hathor) in attendance.

The cult of Osiris dates back to around 2300–2200 BC, and lasted until the end of paganism. He became an important deity throughout the Greco-Roman world through his association with the cult of Isis.

Osiris was venerated throughout Egypt, not least because many towns claimed to be the home of part of his dismembered body after he had been murdered by his brother and antagonist Seth. Abydos, however, is one of the oldest places associated with his name, and includes a symbolic tomb of Osiris (the Osirion) constructed by Rameses II's father Sethy I, and the far older tomb of King Djer (around 2800 BC), which was thought from around 2000 BC to be Osiris's actual tomb, and as such a place of pilgrimage.

Once Osiris began to grow in importance, he was incorporated into a grouping alongside his sisters and brother, Isis, Nephthys, and Seth, and his 'son' Horus. As well as producing an extensive series of mythical stories, the posthumous fathering of Horus acted as a model for the succession of Egyptian kings: the dead king passing the crown to his 'Horus' son. The stories became the basis also for the central hope of immortality in the afterlife.

A complex relationship existed between Osiris and Re. By the time the temples at Abu Simbel were constructed, Osiris could be referred to as 'lord of the universe' or 'king of the gods,' a position akin to that of the sun god.

He was sometimes regarded as the underworld counterpart of Re, or sometimes as the body of Re—the two combining to represent something of a single greater god. The two gods never truly fused, however, and they remained independent deities.

Ptah

Easily recognizable, Ptah is another of the 'old' gods—probably older than Osiris.

As another sheathed human figure, he stands with his feet together and his hands protruding from his sheath. He holds a *was* scepter, forked at the bottom and topped by the ankh and *djed* symbols. He usually wears a close-fitting skullcap, though when he is associated with Osiris, he may be seen with a small disk flanked by two plumes like his neighbor. He wears a distinctive straight beard, rather than the curved beard usually associated with the gods. At his back, he wears a large tassel or counterweight to his broad collar, which is another distinctive feature.

Ptah may stand on a plinth, which resembles both the measuring rod used by workmen and one of the hieroglyphs representing the word *maat*

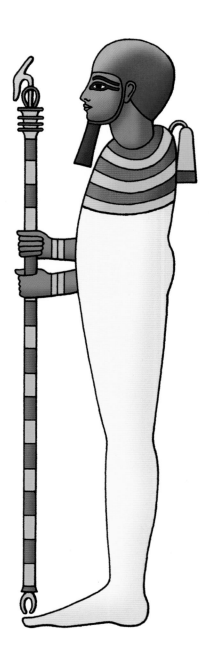

Ptah

(truth). He may also stand on a stepped structure reminiscent of the primeval mound, or, more frequently, he can be seen within an open shrine.

Originally a local god of Memphis, Ptah continued to be closely associated with that city, where his great temple stood—much embellished by Rameses II, as we have noted from the inscription in the Great Temple. His popular veneration spread, however, throughout Egypt. There was a sanctuary to him within the bounds of the great temple to Amun at Karnak, and he was present at a number of Rameses II's other temples in Nubia. Rameses II's son and successor was named Merenptah, 'Ptah's beloved,' which was also an epithet of his father, Sethy I.

Ptah became a member of the Memphite divine 'family'—his consort was the lioness goddess Sekhmet and his son was Nefertem (the god of the lotus blossom that first arose from the primeval waters, according to a version of the creation myths).

That Memphis—where Ptah was 'lord'—became the capital when Egypt was unified must have assisted in his growth to national importance. Indeed, the word 'Egypt' may well be derived indirectly through Greek from Hut-ka-Ptah, 'the Temple of the soul (ka) of Ptah' at Memphis.

Ptah became known as the 'ancient one,' combining within himself the primeval god Nun and his counterpart Naunet (representing the primeval waters)—and his creative spark was seen as being part of all things. In a highly sophisticated manner, Ptah was seen as creating the world through his thought and by his word of command.

Through the absorption of the attributes of other gods from the Memphis area, Ptah also occasionally took on a role as a god of the underworld, but he was more generally regarded as a god who listened to the petitions of the faithful—he was 'the ear that hears.' Shrines to Ptah were often found close to the temples of other gods so that he might help transmit prayers to the temple's deity.

Rameses II

Rameses II appears to have been declared—unusually among the pharaohs—fully divine (rather than having divine attributes) during his lifetime, and he can be seen as such in several of the Nubian temples. In this, Rameses may have been following the earlier example of Amenhotep III in Nubia.

Rameses II

That the deified Rameses was inserted into several reliefs at Abu Simbel suggests that this event occurred some years after his accession.

Re/Re-Horakhty

Throughout this chapter, the name of the sun god Re has been inescapable—especially in combination with other gods, or as the 'father' of several of them. In his midday form, Re-Horakhty, he was the principal god to which the Great Temple at Abu Simbel was dedicated.

Re appears in a large number of forms, the key ones being the scarab of Khepri at dawn, Horakhty at midday, the evening Aten, and the aged ram of the nocturnal underworld. He may also be the disk of the sun itself—protected by an encircling cobra, and often with wings on either side of the disk keeping it aloft in the sky.

During his passage through the celestial seas in his 'day barque' *(mandjet)*, he is sometimes accompanied by his daughter, Maat, or other gods; in the evening, the ram-headed Re would enter the underworld in the 'evening barque' *(mesketet)* before being born again at dawn as Re-Khepri.

Although at various times both Raet and Hathor were considered to be his consort, Re usually appears alone in temples and tombs.

Decorative elements such as sun disks, flying vultures, and yellow bands may also refer to the daily journey of the god toward or through the underworld, especially in tombs. Such a progression may account for the nature of the ceiling in the Great Temple, as may the presence of sun disks on the lintels.

Re/Re-Horakhty

Many ancient architectural forms are linked to Re, including the pyramid and obelisk, and by the time these were first constructed, the kings had adopted the title 'son of Re.' The sun god had effectively become the senior state deity of Egypt and intimately linked to kingship.

The main center of Re's cult was at Heliopolis, but he was worshipped throughout Egypt in both large and small structures (sometimes attached to temples of other gods). During the fourteenth century BC, a special form of Re-Horakhty, the Aten, was introduced into the pantheon, becoming, to an arguable degree, sole god during the reign of Akhenaten (reigned 1377–1337 BC), but was soon discarded in favor of the traditional forms of the sun god in the revived polytheism that followed it.

Such was the longevity and stature of Re that in the early Christian period, prayer texts may occasionally call upon Jesus Christ, the Holy Ghost, and Re.

Re was a universal god in whom many other gods could be incorporated, and he acted in the heavens, the earth, and the underworld. He was a prime mover in the creation—he had emerged from the primeval waters at the beginning of time, and his tears *(remut)*, in one story, created man *(remetj)*.

He directly influenced the earth after that, providing heat and light and causing crops to grow. Each night he regenerated during his travel through the underworld, defeating his archenemy, the snake Apophis, with the help of the gods accompanying him.

The creation of kingship being concurrent with the creation of all things, and Re having been king on earth himself until he was so old that he left for the heavens, his successors—the now-dead kings—accompanied Re on his daily journey.

Satis

The goddess Satis protected the southern border of Egypt, and was closely connected to the Nile and its flood. She appears as a woman wearing the White Crown of Upper Egypt, with antelope horns or plumes attached to it, and a cobra-head uraeus at the front. She wears a sheath dress and may carry an ankh or scepter.

Satis was closely associated with Elephantine Island in Aswan, where her temple was aligned to the star Sirius, which rose at the time of the annual Nile flood. According to some Egyptian traditions, the flood began in this area.

As 'mistress of Elephantine,' Satis was the consort of Khnum and the mother of Anukis, though earlier connections with Montu are known. When Khnum was identified with Re, Satis might become an 'Eye of Re' and take on some of the characteristics of Hathor.

Sekhmet

One of the most fascinating ancient Egyptian deities, Sekhmet was the principal lioness goddess—combining within herself unpredictable, ferocious, and protective attributes.

She appears most often as a woman with the head of a lioness. She wears a long wig topped by a

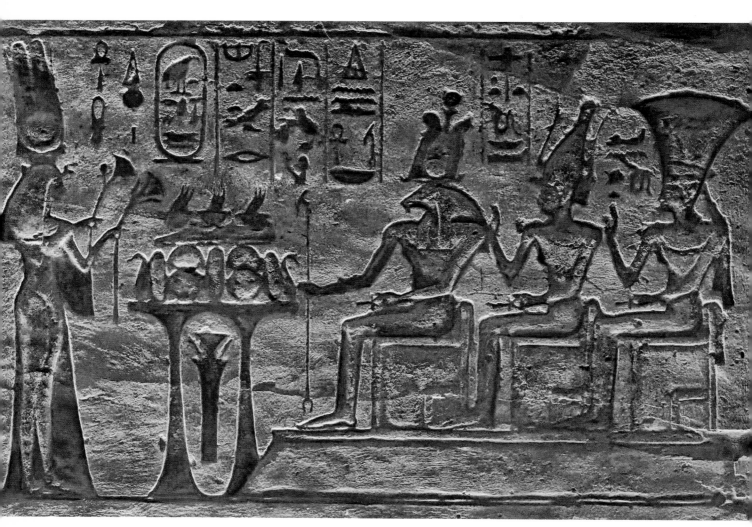

Nefertiry presents flowers to the Elephantine triad of
Khnum, Satis, and Anukis: upper right on the wall
to the left of the sanctuary door, Small Temple.

Sekhmet

solar disk, and a long red dress—perhaps symbolizing Lower Egypt or just her warlike aspect. Over each nipple, she may wear a rosette that is reminiscent of representations of the lion's 'shoulder star' in the constellation of Leo. More rarely, Sekhmet may simply appear as a lioness.

Many statues of Sekhmet—some first uncovered by Belzoni—were discovered in the Temple of Mut south of Amun's temple precinct at Karnak, although all had been moved from the memorial temple of Amenhotep III on the other side of the river, where more continue to be found. These show Sekhmet seated or standing and holding the papyrus scepter associated with Lower Egypt.

The main cult center of the goddess was at Memphis, but she was worshipped in many other places, either on her own or as an aspect of other goddesses. Mut and Sekhmet may thus sometimes be directly fused and wear both the crowns of Egypt.

Sekhmet was the consort of Ptah and mother of Nefertem (the god of the lotus flower that arose at the creation, and of perfumes) at Memphis, and was closely associated with Hathor. She was also linked to Pakhet, the lioness patron of Middle Egypt, and with the cat goddess Bastet.

Sekhmet's name means 'the female powerful one,' in keeping, principally, with her destructive aspect. She was regarded as a daughter of Re, and an eye of the sun god. In myth, when Re (as king on earth) became old and humanity rose up against him, he sent Sekhmet to punish them, which led to something close to their annihilation.

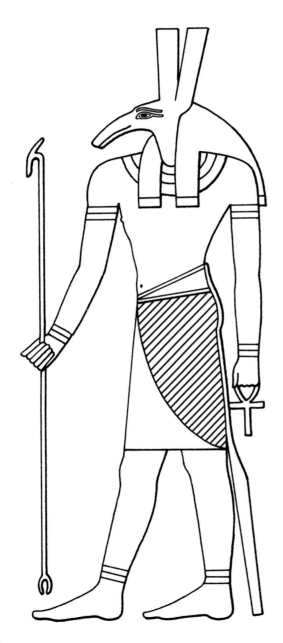

Seth

Her habit of breathing fire against her enemies led to her adoption by Egyptian kings as the patroness of military adventures. In this manner, for example, Sekhmet became the 'smiter of the Nubians.'

The hot winds of the desert were the breath of the goddess, and epidemics, which swept the land periodically, were the 'slaughterers of Sekhmet.'

The other face of Sekhmet, however, was as the fierce, motherly protector of the king. She was also regarded as the goddess who had the power to ward off disease or heal the sick, in her aspect as 'mistress of life.'

Seth

Seth's role among the gods was particularly ambivalent, not least because he represented the forces of chaos, and was the murderer of Osiris.

He was originally represented as a creature with a curved head, tall rectangular ears, and a tail held high. The creature might be seated, or standing, or crouching. Much later, Seth appears in human form, with the extraordinary head of the creature, who sometimes wears the White Crown of Upper Egypt or the Double Crown. He may also be found fused with Horus, symbolically binding Upper and Lower Egypt.

Seth could be represented by many ritually offensive or dangerous animals (for example, the antelope, ass, pig, hippopotamus, crocodile, and certain species of fish). Toward the end of pharaonic Egypt, the god Seth disappeared as a physical representation and is only referred to obliquely, so that he might not have the opportunity to do harm.

The god had cult centers throughout the country, but was often regarded as the patron god of Upper Egypt and a counterbalance to Horus in Lower Egypt. His earliest cult center may have been at Ombos (ancient Nubt, modern Naqada) at the entrance to the desert route through Wadi Hammamat. Indeed, the origins of Seth may have been as a desert deity representing the perceived chaos of that environment in contrast to the ordered and cultivated Nile Valley.

While the Hyksos ruled northern Egypt (1650–1535 BC), Seth was identified with Baal, the storm god of the Canaanites, and rose to be a major god. His increased importance in the Delta and with the Rameses family (including Sethy I, 'the one of Seth') may have stemmed directly from this. Avaris, the Hyksos capital with its temple to Seth, was renewed as the fully developed city of Piramesses under Rameses II.

Seth was the god of violence, chaos, and confusion, the 'Red One'—the personification of evil. He opposed the harmony of *maat*, and represented rebellion and discord. He lurked in the underworld to seize the souls of the dead, and he was behind sickness, disease, unrest, and invasion. His hands caused storms, bad weather, and the raging sea.

Yet he was also the god of strength, cunning, and protection. His scepter weighed 2,000 kilograms (4,500 pounds), and he was the lord of metals. Iron, the hardest metal known in ancient Egypt, was known as 'the bones of Seth.' Hence, many kings associated themselves with his strength, and Rameses II, for example, was described as having fought like Seth at the battle of Qadesh.

That strength, together with that of Horus, was also seen as binding the two lands of Egypt together, and it was Seth's strength and cunning that defeated Apophis every night in the underworld so that Re might rise again.

Seth could also be appealed to in everyday life, and it was to him that Rameses prayed so that the storms that prevented a Hittite bride from entering Egypt might abate.

Seshat

Seshat was the goddess of writing and notation in all their forms, and the patroness of temple and other libraries. She appears in human form and often wears the leopard skin of a high priest over her robe. She also wears a headband knotted at the back of her head, with a tall emblem, of unknown meaning, shaped like a seven-pointed star or rosette on a stick (𐰀). A bow or crescent may appear above this emblem, sometimes topped by two falcon feathers.

She usually holds a palm rib upon which she notches the passing years. This may terminate with the *shen* hieroglyph for infinity (◯). Seshat is sometimes seen associated with the foundation ceremony of temples alongside the king. In this capacity, she carries a mallet and stake and holds the measuring line taut to mark out the building.

Seshat is known from very early in Egyptian history, particularly in this 'stretching the cord' ceremony associated with temple building, though she appears never to have had a temple of her own. She was nonetheless known as 'the mistress of builders.'

The goddess was associated with all forms of counting, whether it was of animals, foreign captives, or the Egyptian population in official censuses. It was Seshat who recorded the regnal years of the king, and his jubilees, on the leaves of the sacred *ished* or *persea* tree.

She was often associated with Thoth as, variously, his consort, sister, or daughter.

Taweret

The name of Taweret, 'the great one,' is another that stretches back to the earliest days of the Egyptian state. She was the protective goddess of pregnancy and childbirth.

Taweret usually appears as a heavily pregnant, standing hippopotamus with hanging breasts. She wears a wig, with a feathered headdress, a low cylindrical 'crown' *(modius)*, or horns, and a solar disk. Her mouth is usually open, with the lips pulled back to reveal her teeth, possibly as a sign of protection. She carries the *sa* symbol of protection (𓋹 —a loop representing the sun rising above the horizon) and an ankh. She may carry a torch to dispel darkness and demons.

She may appear with the head of a cat or a woman, or, as in the Small Temple, she may appear in fully human form.

She was sometimes closely associated with Isis or Hathor (whose headdress she may wear). As Seth was sometimes represented as a hippopotamus, Taweret could be considered his consort, though she was also considered to be the consort of Bes (a complex god

Taweret

noted for his protection of children, pregnant women, and those giving birth).

Naturally, the protective role of Taweret made her a popular goddess throughout Egyptian society, and within the wider Mediterranean world.

Tefnut

Tefnut was the daughter of Atum and the sister/wife of Shu, but is otherwise largely enigmatic. She was most often represented as a lioness or as a woman with a lion's head, though she may also appear in fully human form. She may wear a long wig and a solar disk with a cobra-head uraeus.

The main centers of her worship were Heliopolis and Leontopolis (modern Tell al-Muqdam) in the Delta, where she was worshipped with Shu in the form of a pair of lions.

She was the goddess of moisture but may have had other, deeper roles, including representing the atmosphere of the lower world in the same manner that Shu represented that of the upper world.

In her form as a lioness, Tefnut was an 'Eye of Re,' though in myth she also quarreled with the sun god.

Thoth

Thoth (ancient Egyptian Djehuty) was a moon god of great antiquity who became associated with writing and knowledge.

The god was most often represented as an ibis-headed man, as a baboon, or as an ibis. Unlike the sun-adoring baboons which top the façade of the Great Temple at Abu Simbel, Thoth in his baboon

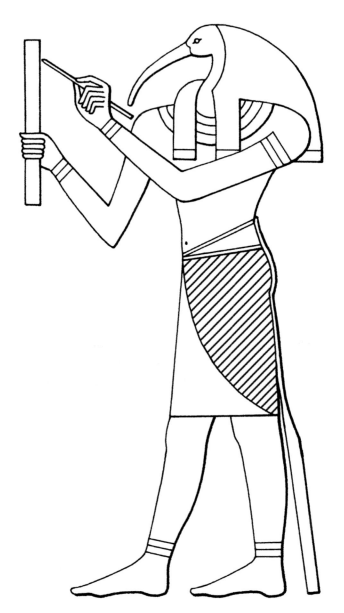

Thoth

form is shown seated, resting on his haunches, and with his arms resting on his knees. Sometimes the lunar disk and crescent rest on top of his head. In the form of an ibis, he may sit, stand, or perch.

His consort was Nehemetawy (a minor goddess worshipped in the temples of Thoth and often depicted nursing an infant on her lap), but he was also associated with the goddess of writing, Seshat, who is sometimes found as his consort or daughter.

The center of the worship of Thoth was at Khemnu (Greek Hermopolis; modern al-Ashmunein)—though it is possible that his worship began in the Delta—and sites associated with him are widespread, stretching from the Western Desert to the Sinai Peninsula.

Royal associations with the god are evident in the names of some pharaohs, including Thutmose ('born of Thoth'), but more general veneration of the god is also clear from the many thousands of mummified ibises and baboons in the Ibeum near Hermopolis and at Saqqara.

Alongside Re and as his son, Thoth crossed the sky. Other gods traveled upon the 'wing' of Thoth on the 'river' of the heavens. In his lunar aspect, he was often placed in juxtaposition to Re, as the 'night sun.'

Thoth protected and served Osiris, and he often acted as a messenger between the gods, bringing about reconciliation between them. Perhaps this latter aspect was related to the belief that Thoth invented writing.

He acted as the scribe to the gods and recorded their divine words and records. As 'lord of time' and 'reckoner of years' he also kept account of passing time, and can often be seen assigning long reigns to the kings of Egypt.

His record-keeping extended to the underworld, and he was to be found before the scales that weighed the heart of the deceased against the feather of Maat, recording the outcome. In this, and in all things, Thoth had a reputation for truth and integrity.

All areas of knowledge came under his patronage, so, unsurprisingly, Thoth supervised magic and kept secrets that were unknown to the other gods.

4 | SAVING ABU SIMBEL

Of all the possible fates that might have befallen the temples at Abu Simbel—including attack, earthquake, burial, or simply wearing away over time—the most improbable for most of its history would surely be drowning.

Ninety-six percent of Egypt is desert, and the vast majority of the population have always lived on the remaining four percent. Herodotus's oft-quoted comment about the Nile Delta, that it was 'the gift of the river,' has often been used subsequently to describe the whole country.

Unsurprisingly, then, by the end of the nineteenth century, Egypt's population was rapidly outgrowing its agricultural resources, and the country could no longer afford to lose arable land during the summer months, or risk the consequences to the modern cotton industry of the annual variability in the flood—too high or too low being equal problems down the ages for Egypt. The decision was taken, consequently, to attempt to regulate the Nile flood by building a dam at the First Cataract in Aswan (between 1899 and 1902).

That first Aswan dam was never intended to store flood water from season to season, but simply to regulate the flow of the Nile through 180 sluice gates, and the height of the dam was deliberately limited due to concerns for the temple at Philae just to the south.

Although the original dam worked well, usage soon outstripped the capacity of the reservoir and the height was raised 5 meters (16 feet) between 1907 and 1912, and a further 9 meters (30 feet) between 1929 and 1933.

After the raising of the dam, the reservoir stretched back to Wadi Halfa in northern Sudan, and the water level rose from 87 to 121 meters (285 to 395 feet).

Despite the archaeological surveys conducted before each raising of the dam, some temples were now partly submerged for most of the year and required consolidation work to strengthen them. In addition, many Nubian villages—dependent upon the thin strip of cultivable land on the riverbanks—began to disappear forever under the waters. Their inhabitants were ultimately to be displaced to Aswan and far beyond.

By 1947, the population of Egypt stood at around 20,000,000—more than twice the population when the first dam was built—and the country's agricultural production was again in danger of failing to keep pace. Consequently, in 1954, shortly after Gamal Abdel Nasser came to power, the decision was made to construct a higher dam—7 kilometers (4 miles) upstream from the first—based on a German design and using financial assistance from a number of western states.

This promise of financial assistance was withdrawn in 1956 due to Nasser's refusal to stop purchasing arms from the Eastern Bloc. In retaliation, Nasser quickly nationalized the Suez Canal and turned to the Soviet Union for assistance, which was delivered in the form of a credit system underwriting the new High Dam and 2,000 engineers and technicians, who would work alongside a 30,000-strong Egyptian workforce.

The foundation stone of the new dam was laid in January 1960, the beginning of a structure 3,600 meters long and 100 meters high (11,810 feet long and 328 feet high). The dam consists of a clay core with rock and sand fill faced with concrete—representing 17 times the volume of material used in the construction of the Great Pyramid at Giza.

The reservoir—known today as Lake Nasser—would stretch 500 kilometers (310 miles) to the south (a relatively small part of that in Sudan), and vary between 5 and 35 kilometers (3 and 22 miles) wide, with an average width of 10 kilometers (6 miles). The archaeological world immediately saw the danger to the many sites in Nubia that had hugged the river channel for centuries.

From 1955, UNESCO (the United Nations Educational, Scientific and Cultural Organization) and Egypt's Center of Documentation on Ancient Egypt cooperated to record Nubian archaeological sites in advance of plans to build the High Dam, and it was quickly realized that the effects of the dam would be catastrophic from the perspective of cultural heritage.

As a result, in 1958, the American ambassador to Egypt, Raymond Hare, and the director of the Metropolitan Museum, James Rorimer, approached Egypt's minister of culture, Tharwat Okasha, to inquire whether the United States might purchase one or two threatened temples from the Egyptian government. Equally concerned by the potential calamity, Dr. Okasha was spurred forward to develop plans for the possible rescue of 17 temples between Aswan and Wadi Halfa.

Early in 1959, Okasha proposed that UNESCO should mount an international effort, supported financially by Egypt and a global campaign for funding. UNESCO's director-general, Vittorino Veronese, was quickly convinced, and President Nasser followed suit by agreeing that Egypt would underwrite one-third of the cost.

The resulting plan consisted of three parts: the recording of all monuments in the threatened area; the excavation, or re-excavation, of all known archaeological sites; and the transfer of all threatened temples to safety. This plan was again supported by UNESCO.

As early as 1960, salvage work began—including the dismantling of the temples at Debod and Taffeh, which were stored on Elephantine Island at Aswan—but Abu Simbel remained at the top of the agenda, followed by a plan to move the temples at Philae to safety.

The Egyptian government committed 3,500,000 Egyptian pounds, within a seven-year time frame, to rescue the Abu Simbel temples, and UNESCO began the process of building cooperation and securing financial support for the project.

French engineers suggested leaving the temples in place and building a high concrete wall in front of them, but the Italian engineer Piero Gazzolo, through the Italian engineering company Italconsult, proposed transferring the temples to higher ground. A modified form of Gazzolo's idea (he had suggested moving the temples in one piece) was accepted, and on 20 June 1961 the Swedish engineering company Vattenbyggnadsbyrån (VBB), who had modified the Italian plan, was granted the contract to undertake the work. VBB estimated the cost at 36,000,000 dollars; the final cost was around 40,000,000 dollars. An international consortium of contractors—Joint Venture Abu Simbel—carried out the work.

The accepted plan was deceptively simple: to cut the temple into large blocks, transfer these to a storage area, and rebuild the temple at a greater height above the lake in an appropriate setting. In addition, the temples were to be rebuilt in exactly the same configuration, alignment to the cardinal points, and distance from one another.

First, when work began in 1964, the temples had to be protected from the already rising waters of the lake (an average vertical increase at Abu Simbel of 8 meters [26 feet] in 1964, and a further 5 meters [16 feet] in 1965). There was a very real danger that the temples would be severely damaged by the rising water before they could be fully dismantled in 1966.

A cofferdam was constructed in front of the temples and continuous pumping kept the water at bay. In addition, steel scaffolding was inserted in each of the temples, and the façades were covered with protective sand, with a steel culvert inserted to provide access to the Great Temple. Screens were also inserted above the façades.

All this protection—especially the steel framework within the temples—was essential, as the cliffs above the temples were to be entirely removed before the temples were carved into blocks.

The equipment available on site did not allow the blocks cut from the temple halls to exceed 20 metric tons (21 tons), and those from the façade 30 metric tons (33 tons). While visitors may feel that they are surrounded by solid rock in the temples, the walls of the rebuilt temple are only about 80 centimeters (32 inches) deep, and those of the façade between 60 and 120 centimeters (24 and 47 inches).

Opposite: Crews using long saws to cut up the upper part of the Great Temple façade.

The face of Rameses II as it was removed in one piece from the façade of the Great Temple.

Where the cuts were to be made was decided by the engineers and archaeologists together, with due consideration for the fracture risks associated with elongated or very heavy blocks. The process was guided by detailed drawings of the temples, and each block was meticulously planned—no cut could be made across the faces of statues or intricate parts of decorated surfaces.

Where the cuts would be visible, they were made with handsaws. Where they would not be seen—behind the blocks—chainsaws were used. Just as the ancient Egyptians would have done, the roof blocks were divided by boring and splitting.

When free from their surroundings, two to four steel rods were inserted into the top of each block that allowed vertical lifting without the equipment coming into direct contact with the sandstone. Each block was placed on a low-loader, transported to an open storage area (only one heavy rain shower occurred during the whole process), and later moved to the new temple site to be placed in its final position.

No block was lost or suffered more than superficial damage.

The final positioning of the temples in relation to each other remained the same—though both temples were moved 208 meters (682 feet) to the northwest. The Great Temple now stands 65 meters (213 feet), and the Small Temple 67 meters (220 feet), above their original locations.

The reassembled walls and façade are essentially self-supporting but are braced to the rear by concrete structures (except behind the sloping façade, these structures carry no load). The partition walls and columns are self-supporting but braced at the roof, and the roofs are supported by an overlying concrete structure to which the blocks are tied by closely spaced anchor bars.

In the final stages, restorers from the Egyptian Antiquities Department filled the gaps between the blocks with natural sandstone mortar bound with resin, lime, or cement.

Both temples were covered by concrete domes that took the strain of the artificial hills above, allowed engineers and archaeologists to inspect and repair the rear of the structures, and facilitated the lighting and ventilation of the temples. The ventilation, in particular, provides a comfortable environment for the visitor as well as minimizing potentially harmful humidity. The larger dome over the Great Temple has a free span of 59 meters (194 feet) and a height of 26 meters (85 feet). The smaller dome has a free span of 24 meters (79 feet) and a height of 20 meters (66 feet).

The final stage of the project was to set the rescued temples into an appropriate landscape reminiscent of, but not copying, the original cliffside location. By this stage, the funds associated with the Abu Simbel project were beginning to run out, which meant that the engineers had to apply almost as much ingenuity to the landscaping as they had to the assembly of the temples in their new location.

The cliff faces around the temples are constructed of sandstone blocks; the gaps are filled using mortar that resembles the temple blocks. These have been hand-chiseled to look like natural rock (ably assisted subsequently by Nubian sandstorms).

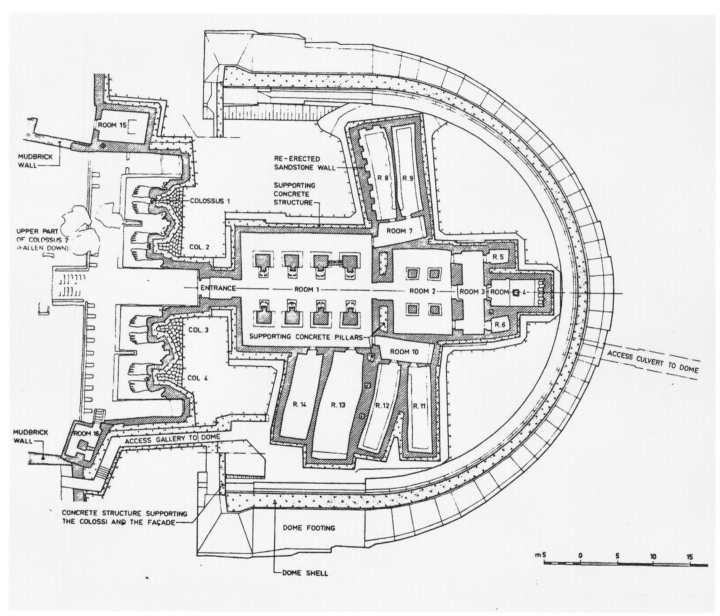

Plan of the domed structure covering the Great Temple showing the concrete support for the walls of the temple.

The rear of the new temple structure also presented a challenge. After several trial attempts, the VBB engineers decided that over such a large area it would not be possible to recreate a natural-looking desert landscape, so they designed stylized hills that did not detract from the main features of the temples that visitors would come to see.

The work of reassembling the temples, which had begun on 26 January 1966, finished with the last block from the façade of the Great Temple placed on 9 September 1967, 14 days ahead of schedule.

The new temple site was inaugurated in the presence of President Nasser, and many national and international dignitaries, on 22 September 1968.

FURTHER READING

This book is composed of condensed versions of some of the chapters of my *Abu Simbel and the Nubian Temples*. The original book contains much more information on the discovery of the Abu Simbel temples and the gods and goddesses associated with them, together with chapters on Rameses II's legacy within Egypt and his military campaigns. The book also describes the other temples to be seen around Lake Nasser between Philae and Abu Simbel.

As accessible overviews of the pharaonic period, I recommend Aidan Dodson's *Monarchs of the Nile* and the perennial *Atlas of Ancient Egypt* by John Baines and Jaromír Málek.

Thames and Hudson's *The Complete . . .* series of titles about ancient Egypt are both readable and useful—particularly, in the areas covered by this book, Richard Wilkinson's *The Complete Gods and Goddesses of Ancient Egypt* and *The Complete Temples of Ancient Egypt*, and Steven Snape's *The Complete Cities of Ancient Egypt*.

On ancient Nubia and its monuments, I highly recommend Jocelyn Gohary's invaluable *Guide to the Nubian Monuments on Lake Nasser* and the excellent *Ancient Nubia: African Kingdoms on the Nile* edited by Marjorie Fisher, Peter Lacovara, Salima Ikram, and Sue D'Auria.

Plan for cutting up the façade of the Great Temple without crossing critical architectural features.

Image Credits

Temple Plans: Franck Monnier

Drawings: Dominique Navarro

Maps: Cherif Abdullah/AUC Press

Plans on pages 85 and 86: Courtesy of Sweco AB

Hieroglyphs were inserted into the text using EZGlyph Pro

Photographs by the author, except: The New York Public Library Digital Collection, pages 3 and 24–25; Sweco AB, pages 82–83